THE CULTURE SECRET

WORKBOOK

The Ultimate Guide to Empower People and
Companies No Matter What You Sell

DR. DAVID VIK

GREENLEAF
BOOK GROUP PRESS

Published by Greenleaf Book Group Press
Austin, Texas
www.greenleafbookgroup.com

Copyright ©2013 David Vik
All rights reserved.

No part of this book may be reproduced, stored in a retrieval system, or transmitted by any means, electronic, mechanical, photocopying, recording, or otherwise, without written permission from the publisher.

Distributed by Greenleaf Book Group LLC
For ordering information or special discounts for bulk purchases, please contact Greenleaf Book Group LLC at PO Box 91869, Austin, TX 78709, 512.891.6100.

Design and composition by Greenleaf Book Group LLC
Cover design by Greenleaf Book Group LLC

Publisher's Cataloging-In-Publication Data
(Prepared by The Donohue Group, Inc.)
Vik, David.
   The culture secret workbook : the ultimate guide to empower people and companies no matter what you sell / David Vik.—1st ed.
   p. ; cm.
   Issued also as an ebook.
   ISBN: 978-1-62634-015-2

   1. Employee empowerment—Problems, exercises, etc. 2. Employee retention—Problems, exercises, etc. 3. Corporate culture—Problems, exercises, etc. I. Title.

HD50.5 .V552 2013
658.4/02/076   2013934671

Part of the Tree Neutral® program, which offsets the number of trees consumed in the production and printing of this book by taking proactive steps, such as planting trees in direct proportion to the number of trees used: www.treeneutral.com

Printed in the United States of America on acid-free paper

13 14 15 16 17   10 9 8 7 6 5 4 3 2 1

First Edition

CONTENTS

v   **Welcome to *The Culture Secret Workbook***

1   **Chapter 1: Vision**
This Is What We Are Doing

14   **Chapter 2: Purpose**
This Is Why We Are Doing It

25   **Chapter 3: Business Model**
This Is What Will Fuel Us

37   **Chapter 4: Unique/WOW Factors**
This Is What Makes Us Stand Out

47   **Chapter 5: Values**
This Is What We Care About

57   **Chapter 6: Culture**
This Is What Is and What Could Be

71   **Chapter 7: Leadership**
This Is Empowering and Passing the Torch

81   **Chapter 8: Human Resources/Human Empowerment**
This Is the Group of Champions

89   **Chapter 9: Customers and Customer Service**
This Is Essential to the Process

98   **Chapter 10: Brand**
This Is What They Say About Us

105   **Chapter 11: Experience and the Emotional Connection**
This Is the Pot of Gold if We Do It Right

113   **Congratulations!**

Welcome to *The Culture Secret Workbook*!

Congratulations for making this investment in your company's Culture—one that will secure the successful future of your employees and company! This workbook is designed to help your employees and company to reach their full potential.

If you follow the steps outlined in the eleven sections of this workbook, you can help secure your company's success by creating a Culture that not only attracts loyal employees and customers, but also ensures that you have made the shift to the Information Age and are in alignment with the wants, needs, and demands of employees and customers.

This workbook contains some material from the book *The Culture Secret*, plus new information, examples, and exercises that will help you create your own unique Culture. By reading about how other companies have created a great Culture and by going through the process yourself through the exercises included in each section, you'll get a better "feel" for what it takes to create your own unique Culture.

In the first five sections, you'll learn how to come up with a great Vision, Purpose, Business Model, Unique/WOW Factors, and Values. These are the five crucial structures that will create the foundation of your Culture, and you'll read about how other companies went through the thought and decision-making process to create their own unique Culture. Creating your own unique Culture structures will require a good amount of creation and alignment, so the first five sections of this workbook are therefore longer than the last six, which have been created to bring your Culture to life!

The sixth section focuses on how these structures come together to form the Culture itself. And in the final five sections, you'll look at five key aspects of Culture—Leadership; Human Empowerment; Customers and Customer Service; Brand; and Experience and the Emotional Connection—and how you can implement them in your company in a way that supports a great and unique company Culture.

Have fun as you work through these sections, and enjoy creating your unique Culture—the rewards are incredible for your employees, customers, and company, to say the least!

Love,
Doc

1
VISION

This is what we are doing.

Objective:

To create a great Vision for your company. The Vision is the starting point of a great Culture. It will be an important part of your Culture blueprint for what you are going to create. The Vision will also act as a North Star or a guiding light that will help align the thoughts, decisions, and actions of employees.

McPherson Aerosol Can Company was stuck in a terrible rut. It wanted to grow, but the firm's leaders knew they could only do so much with the aerosol cans they manufactured—change the nozzle, tweak the can shape, or put different liquids inside. Because the company wasn't growing, employees couldn't move up. Morale was poor. Worse, overseas companies had recently come to market with less expensive aerosol cans, meaning that margins were tighter than ever.

But one day, a young employee went to his boss with an idea. He thought that if the company widened the scope of products it made, new markets would open up to it. Thus, he suggested to his boss that the company change its name from McPherson Aerosol Can Company to McPherson Container Corporation. Company leaders, desperate for a new approach, agreed to implement it. Along with the new name came a new Vision: *"We Contain All Liquids, Solids, and Gases."*

With its new, wider Vision, the company found it had opened up virtually every market that had to do with a container. From milk cartons, paint cans, and cardboard boxes to plastic bags and shipping containers, there was virtually no end to the products that needed to be contained. Meanwhile, the rest of the container industry was stuck in the past. With new designs and enhanced capabilities, the McPherson Container Corporation took advantage of all kinds of innovation and improvements. And no longer were employees stuck in a dead-end job. Now they had a vision—of containing all kinds of things. Many frontline employees felt empowered to share ideas with their own bosses.

That's the power a change in Vision can have on a company. To reap these same benefits, you don't need to change your company's name like McPherson did, but you do need to take a closer look at your Vision, which is the starting point of a great Culture.

> ### A Vision . . .
>
> - Expresses the focus of what your company does or wants to become
>
> or
>
> - Is what you want to deliver
>
> and
>
> - Fulfills your employees
> - Is in alignment with the Information Age
> - Is in alignment with the wants, needs, and demands of the customer and employee.

Having a Vision of what you want to create gives you clarity. Your Vision has to be bigger than yourself and the company, and it has to be about more than just making money. Employees can get behind a vision of making money for a little while, but if the money isn't spread around, it soon loses its luster.

The Vision answers the question of *what* your company does, but it should also be about the *benefits* of what you provide. So basically, you know *what* your company does, but you need to figure out what that *what* does to benefit the customer.

Say you're a law firm. *What* you do is make contracts. But your Vision should go beyond that and explain the ultimate benefit of *what* you're doing. Your law firm, with its contracts, provides certainty, now and in the future for your clients or customers, so the Vision might be "*Securing Your Future.*" If you establish this Vision as the North Star that guides you and your employees, you'll open a lot of doors, opportunities, and possibilities in how you will secure the future of your clients.

Here's another example of how a change in Vision can bring new focus: Suppose you owned a limousine company whose Vision was based on this *what*: "*Taking People from Here to There.*" Imagine if this company switched its Vision to describe how it benefited the customer, making it this instead: "*Making Every Occasion Special.*" I'd bet that this Vision would change the way people did things; employees would be looking toward a new North Star. Realizing that their job was to be a part of the special moments in their customers' lives—not just to get them from point A to point B—they'd start asking themselves, "How can I help make this ride an occasion, and make it as special as possible?" By simply embracing this new Vision, you'd have a different and far more popular and successful business.

Though many Visions will center around the company's offerings, some Visions may be stronger if focused on *how* that product, service, or knowledge is delivered. This is especially true if you are in the services business or if you sell a commodity. Since a service or a commodity isn't proprietary, you need to be Unique/WOW in your delivery (we'll talk more about this in section 4). But for now, think about how your product, service, or knowledge can be delivered differently and what you want your customers to experience. When this becomes the basis for your Vision, you'll rise above the rest.

It is also important that a Vision empowers employees, not restricts them, which is why, even though the Vision is about "what," it shouldn't be about *precisely* "what." Leave it open-ended. Give the employees their much-needed want and desire: autonomy in how they carry out the Vision. If you inspire them and let them do their thing, and align with the Vision in their own way, they'll come back with better ideas and solutions than you could've imagined.

Of course, your company probably already has a Vision of some kind. Most believe that their company has one; generally, however, employees have been unable to share it with me for one of the following reasons:

- They don't know what it is.
- They don't understand it.
- They are familiar with the Vision but cannot repeat it because it is too long or complicated to remember.
- The Vision is muddled in a long-winded mission statement that makes little sense to them.

Luckily, these challenges can be remedied. You can create a Vision that is simple, repeatable, and well understood by the employees so they can be in alignment with it.

GREAT VISIONS FROM THE REAL WORLD

A Vision can transform your culture, or it can just sit there doing nothing. Let's look at some real-world examples. (I've bolded the Vision part of these; we'll cover the second part—Purpose—in the next section).

Google

"**To organize the world's information** and make it universally accessible and useful."

Notice that Google doesn't bother saying precisely how it's going to achieve its Vision. Doing so would box employees in and thwart creativity. Instead, it just says *what* it is going to do.

Apple

"To make a contribution to the world by **making tools for the mind** that advance humankind."

Another great one. Apple's Vision is to make tools for the mind—no mention of computers, phones, tablets, or TVs.

Zappos

"**Delivering happiness** to customers, employees, and vendors."

The Vision at Zappos is big, simple, and empowering. Notice it includes everyone in the chain—the company's goal is to create a win-win-win that leaves everyone happy.

A CLOUDY VISION

Blockbuster

Here's what you get when you Google Blockbuster's Vision:

"At Blockbuster, diversity means valuing differences. It's a corporate value that must be continually developed, embraced, and incorporated into the way we do business."

Here's where things get sticky. Diversity is a great goal, but how do these two sentences tell employees what the company wants to do or deliver? This Vision is foggy and too long. And if one were asked to bold the part of this statement that is the Vision, it would be nearly impossible.

THE ESSENCE OF A GREAT VISION

I hope you're starting to see some common threads. Let's recap some of the crucial characteristics of a great Vision.

> It is **inspiring** (it "thinks big").
> It is **concise, memorable, and easy to repeat.**
> It explains the **benefits of what you provide or how you provide it.**
> It is **supportive of future growth, possibilities, and opportunities.**
> It is **about more than money.**
> It is **likely to attract customers** *and* **employees.**

You also want to tie a Purpose to your Vision, and we'll discuss that in depth in the next section. For now, just remember that your Vision needs to be short enough to allow folks to remember it and the Purpose, too.

But What About Our Mission Statement?

Lots of other books will encourage you to come up with a mission statement, and you may very well already have a mission statement. But I encourage you to ditch it.

I recently gave a talk at one of the world's largest car rental companies. I asked everyone what their company's Vision was. They told me they didn't have a Vision, but they had a mission statement. It was 70 words long and printed on a 4' x 6' poster that they all passed every day. Yet no one could remember even two words of it. Without a clear, motivating, memorable Vision, this company was left competing on price, with employees grinding out their careers day by day.

Here is Blockbuster's mission statement:

> Our corporate mission is to provide our customers with the most convenient access to media entertainment, including movie and game entertainment delivered through multiple distribution channels such as our stores, by mail, vending and kiosks, online and at home. We believe Blockbuster offers customers a value-prices entertainment experience, combining the broad product depth of a specialty retailer with local neighborhood convenience.

Here's the challenge: it's way too long, no one could ever repeat it (let alone remember it), and it impedes creativity and reinvention and is too specific on "how" entertainment will be provided, because the "how" will change over time.

In the space below, see if you can turn Blockbuster's mission statement into a compelling, motivating, repeatable Vision:

_____

_____

How long is your new Vision? See if you can get it down to six words:

_____

PRACTICE

Before we move on to creating your new vision statement, let's try some examples. Below are a few fictional companies that have less than optimal Vision statements. Let's see how they can craft a new, better Vision. Keep in mind that we want these visions to be a "KISS"—Keep It Simple, Sweetie. Ideally, the vision should be six words or less.

1. Stan's Fruit Stand

The current Vision: Stanley Smith owns a medium-sized fruit stand, and employs about five people. Stan's set his Vision as *"To become the biggest fruit stand chain in the world."*

The challenge: This Vision will not attract employees or customers. Surely not many employees care much about working for the biggest fruit stand in the world, nor do customers care whether Stan's stand is bigger than all his competitors' stands. With this Vision, Stan is thinking big about the future, and that's good, but he needs to think about *what* he's delivering to customers and employees, how these offerings will attract and benefit them, and how that's going to get him where he wants to go.

A better Vision: Take a look at these three options and select the one you think works best as a new Vision for Stan:

> **A.** Building the healthiest workforce in town.
> **B.** Providing the finest-quality fresh organic fruits and vegetables.
> **C.** Bringing our community a wide selection of potatoes.

That's right! Option **B**—*"Providing the finest-quality fresh organic fruits and vegetables"*—is the best Vision for Stan. Option **A** will appeal to employees, but probably not to customers. And option **C** is far too limiting. But option **B** has the potential to draw customers and employees, and it can serve as a litmus test against which every person on his team measures his or her efforts and the products they're selling. Stan currently offers fruits and vegetables only, so this is an appropriate Vision, but he may need to revisit it if his offerings change in the future. Say customers start asking for free-range chicken or loaves of flaxseed bread. He would be smart to widen his offerings and update the company's Vision to *"Providing the finest-quality fresh organic foods."*

Can you think of any other possible Visions for Stan's Fruit Stand? What's a Vision that would work for Stan if he wanted to focus on organic, sustainably harvested produce without closing the door to future possibilities and opportunities?

_____

_____

2. Shair

The current Vision: The two founders of Shair created a website and a mobile app that allows users to access and share movie-related content. They've now hired five employees and are just starting to think about their Vision. Their first idea is something like "*We deliver the latest news and content to movie buffs around the world, giving users a chance to share their opinions; access trailers, showtimes, and reviews; read breaking movie news; and find out what their friends are watching.*"

The challenge: As in the previous example, this Vision is far too long. It doesn't really "roll off your tongue." It also severely limits where the company can go in the future. And while the list of features may attract some customers, employees probably won't be thrilled about simply executing a list of services or being boxed into a space of movies only.

A better Vision: Take a look at these three options and select the one you think works best as a new Vision for Shair:

> **A.** Bringing people closer to the magic of entertainment.
> **B.** Your ticket to this week's hottest flicks.
> **C.** To give our customers all Tom Cruise, all the time.

You guessed it—*Bringing people closer to the magic of entertainment* is the best. It's a wide, big-thinking vision that will attract more than just movie buffs. It will also attract employees who are stoked to help customers have the best experience possible and open up all other entertainment opportunities in its future. This new Vision can also scale to many other areas of entertainment, whether they decide to get into live music shows or NASCAR. The Vision is not six words or less, but it's close enough to work. You can even pare it down to "Bringing people closer to entertainment" if you want, but "magic" is pretty attractive. Have fun, and make sure it will "roll off your tongue."

Now try coming up with your own Vision for Shair:

_____

_____

3. Northeastern Data

The current Vision: Northeastern, a midsized data-storage company, has this Vision: "*To make all our employees independently wealthy.*"

The challenge: This Vision attracts employees, but will it attract customers? Probably not. The customer will wonder what's in it for them. Will they be the ones losing out in the company's quest to grow its employees' personal wealth?

A better Vision: Take a look at these three options and select the one you think works best as a new Vision for Northeastern Data:

> **A.** Protecting what matters.
> **B.** Protecting your MacBook Air.
> **C.** Protecting our customers' computer data with high-quality storage systems.

Yep, Option **A** is best. This wider Vision explains the benefits of the company's offerings, and it could open up all kinds of data-storage opportunities and possibilities. Using "*Protecting what matters*" as its North Star, the company could offer its customers secure storage and backup of all kinds of data (pictures, family recipes, genealogy projects, health records, etc.) on any electronic device (including all computers, cell phones, and tablets). Option **C** is a bit long and only encompasses the customer's computer. And **B** will only protect your MacBook Air.

Can you think of another possible Vision for a data-storage company like Northeastern?

_____

_____

DOC'S PRESCRIPTION: CREATE YOUR VISION

Now it's time to start thinking about your own Vision. First write *what* your company offers.

_____

_____

Now write down *what* that does to benefit the customer.

_____

_____

If you have a Vision currently, write it on the lines below. (This could also be your mission statement.)

_____

_____

How many words is it? _____

Do most of your employees know it? _____

Does it inspire people at all levels in your organization? If so, how? If not, why not?

_____

_____

Is it clear, or is it confusing? How so?

_____

_____

Does it accurately describe what you do? How so?

_____

_____

Would you characterize this Vision as "big thinking," or does it limit the company's future? Explain.

_____

_____

What do you think is right about it?

_____

_____

What do you think is wrong about it?

_____

_____

Chances are, your Vision could use some updating. Follow these six steps to see if you can create a new, improved Vision.

Step 1: Get Your "What" Down.

Write out all the services, products, or knowledge that your company currently provides. As you do, look for an overall theme that goes beyond the specifics of your offerings.

_____

_____

_____

_____

Step 2: Think Big.

Now picture what your company might be doing in ten years. What realities may change? What markets might you expand into? Let your imagination go and write out a few possibilities, even if they seem implausible at the moment.

_____

_____

_____

_____

Step 3: Consider Customers.

When a customer walks into your store, calls you up, or navigates to your website, what is he or she looking for? Think beyond the product or service itself. What emotions, experiences, or improvements are you supporting?

_____

_____

_____

_____

Step 4: Consider Employees.

Here's where Vision makes its direct connection with company culture. What is it that keeps your employees working for you? What aspects of the work they do are fulfilling, exciting, or groundbreaking?

_____

_____

_____

_____

Step 5: Write the First Draft of Your Vision.

Review your answers to the previous four questions and come up with one or two ideas for a Vision. Write them here.

_____

_____

_____

_____

Step 6: Refine.

Now discuss the first try (or tries) and try to edit it into a Vision that's six words or less. Write your Vision here.

_____

THE VISION CHECKLIST

I hope you came up with a terrific new Vision for your company that you're excited to share. Real quick, let's take it through a checklist.

Our new Vision . . .

- ☐ is clear
- ☐ is memorable
- ☐ is repeatable
- ☐ is big
- ☐ doesn't limit future opportunities
- ☐ attracts employees
- ☐ supports employees' autonomy and creativity
- ☐ attracts customers

Yes to all? Great! You have a new Vision.

IMPLEMENTING YOUR VISION

It's important to remember that your Vision isn't going to do any good if no one knows it, remembers it, or can repeat it. It's just as important that your employees know the Vision as it is *what* you do. Your Vision should be what everyone, from top to bottom, works toward every day. If everyone has the Vision on their minds, the organization and its culture remain focused and positive, and plenty of opportunities for growth and reinvention will follow. In the next section, we'll be talking about how to define your **Purpose**—this is the "why" to the Vision's "what." Keeping them both top of mind is critical, and we'll cover how to do that after our discussion of Purpose. The Vision should act as the North Star to the creation, delivery, and reinvention of all future offerings; the Purpose, discussed in the next section, will serve to be the motivation behind it.

Don't be discouraged if your Vision stops looking as good as it did after a few weeks. You may need to keep honing it down until the final Vision is clear. It often takes a few tries before you come up with a Vision that clicks for everybody—most importantly the employees and customers.

Hopefully you've future-proofed your Vision, and it will last for years to come, but every now and then you'll need to reevaluate it and make sure it still serves to empower your employees and attracts customers, leading your company to success.

2
PURPOSE

This is why we are doing it.

Objective:

To create a Purpose that's aligned with your Vision. Employees will be attracted to, support, and identify with a compelling company Purpose, and it's their passion that will help create the experiences that your customers will receive.

McPherson Container Corporation had seen great success after establishing its new Vision: *"We Contain All Liquids, Solids, and Gases."* Employees and customers alike now had a clear idea of what the company did, and this Vision had opened many new avenues. Employees looked at this Vision and used it as their North Star—it guided everything they did.

Yet, leaders at McPherson understood that employees also needed to understand *why* the company was bothering to contain liquids, solids, and gases. And it had to be about more than turning a profit—ultimately, a monetary goal would do little to inspire employees to work hard or to convince customers to buy consistently and spread the word about the company.

So, they decided to align a Purpose with the Vision—*"**Helping the World We Live In.**"* They explained that McPherson's ultimate aim was to help the world and the environment we live in; it would thus work to contain its liquids, solids, and gases in a safe, responsible way. Now, not only did employees have a North Star to guide them with their Vision; they also had a *reason* to follow the North Star with their Purpose. This Purpose attracted more employees who wanted to create environmentally friendly containers, opening up even more possibilities and opportunities. And it put passion into employees' efforts and showed them that they were working toward something that was bigger than themselves or the company. Because of the staff's motivation, McPherson's customers had great experiences and developed their own allegiance to the company.

If the first step in building a Culture is to let people know *what* you are doing (your Vision), it makes sense that the second step is to let them know *why* you are doing it. That's where Purpose comes in; it is the reason *why* you are doing *what* you are doing.

Forward-thinking companies do more than make money. They have a Purpose—they want to change the world, in some way!

- Sam Walton explained the Purpose behind Walmart this way: "If we work together, we'll lower the cost of living for everyone—we'll give the world an opportunity to see what it's like to save and have a better life."
- Coca-Cola's Purpose is "To refresh the world; to inspire moments of optimism and happiness; to create value and make a difference."
- Henry Ford's early Purpose for his company was "To democratize the automobile."

It is common for people to want their lives to be connected to something that serves a higher Purpose than themselves. I believe working for a higher Purpose is in our DNA, and when you tap into that impulse by creating a compelling Purpose, you'll inspire, motivate, and help put passion into the Culture.

Some companies direct their energies toward a lesser Purpose—rewards, for instance. But ultimately, it is the big, fulfilling Purposes that energize and empower employees. Let's go back to the example of the limousine company with a Vision of *"Making Every Occasion Special."* What might this company's Purpose be? Definitely not *"To Make a Profit"* or *"To Keep Our Employees in a Job."* Who's going to be inspired and motivated by that? Instead, it might establish this Purpose: *"Because Everyone Matters."* It's simple but powerful. It tells employees that their job is meaningful because they are showing each customer that he or she is important, and that they matter. The employee with this Purpose will be much more likely to go the extra mile—to have flowers waiting for customers in the limo, or to simply give them a big, genuine smile and call them by name. And, of course, customers will appreciate being the sole focus of the company's Purpose.

And what about the law firm whose Vision was *"Securing Your Future"*? What if its Purpose were *"To Provide Peace of Mind"*? In addition to energizing employees, this Purpose shows clients that they don't have to worry about legal technicalities or stress about costs, because all the thoughts, decisions, and actions of the employees will align their internal processes and procedures to the firm's ultimate Purpose: **"to provide peace of mind."** The answers to questions like "How much will it cost?" and "How long will it take?" will be "baked into" the firm's DNA. The clients will appreciate this firm for keeping *their* best interests—not its own—in mind.

Without a Purpose, employees feel that they are wasting their time, and customers show less devotion in doing business with you. But a great Purpose extends far beyond a company's walls and shows everyone that this organization is working to change the world, while making the world a better place—whether they're taking care of people, fostering relationships, or saving the planet.

GREAT PURPOSES FROM THE REAL WORLD

Let's now check out the Purpose part of the statements from the companies we highlighted in the previous section. Notice how each one's Purpose complements and supplements its Vision.

Google

"To organize the world's information and **make it universally accessible and useful.**"

Organizing the world's information would serve no point if no one could use it or access it. So Google's Purpose is to "**make it universally accessible and useful.**"

Apple

"**To make a contribution to the world** by making tools for the mind **that advance humankind.**"

"**To make a contribution to the world**" is a pretty compelling Purpose, and appending the phrase, "**that advance humankind**" adds a big focus to how Apple makes it "tools." How can the company advance humankind if its tools are difficult to use? It can't. Apple actually has a **Purpose–Vision–Purpose sandwich,** where Vision forms the delicious filling between the two slices of Purpose bread (or pita pocket or ciabatta or what have you). Brilliant!

Zappos

"**Delivering happiness** to customers, employees, and vendors."

Zappos's Vision of "**Delivering happiness**" happens to work equally well for its Purpose. Hey, if you are already Delivering happiness, not a lot of other Purposes can top that! So, if your Vision doubles as a Purpose, that's great!

A CLOUDY PURPOSE

Blockbuster

Using the same text that came up when we Googled Blockbuster's Vision, we see that there doesn't seem to be any Purpose in it—or if there is, it's pretty foggy:

"At Blockbuster, diversity means valuing differences. It's a corporate value that must be continually developed, embraced, and incorporated into the way we do business."

Instead of coming up with this impenetrable cloud of words, the company would have, most likely, been better off with a Vision and Purpose that stated: "*Delivering entertainment to the world, accessible to all.*"

THE ESSENCE OF A GREAT VISION

We can now outline some of the crucial features of a great Purpose (several of which are the same as for great Visions).

It is **concise, memorable, and easy to repeat.**

It lends a **greater meaning to your offerings.**

It **extends beyond the walls of your company.**

It makes employees **passionate, inspires them, and gives them a reason to want to come to work.**

It **attracts loyal customers.**

PRACTICE

To help you get even more comfortable with the concept of Purpose, let's go back to our three example companies from the Vision section. We helped them move to a better Vision; now let's see if we can't come up with a Purpose that complements that Vision. Remember, we want these to be just as memorable and repeatable as the Vision—a KISS that's around six words.

1. Stan's Fruit Stand

Stan's Vision: For Stan's fruit stand, we said that a good Vision might be **"Providing the finest-quality fresh organic fruits and vegetables."**

Stan's Purpose: What is the *why* behind the *what* of Stan's Vision? Select the one you think works best:

> **A.** To help put fiber in your diet.
> **B.** Because in today's world, the food industry succeeds by selling an increasingly obese population unhealthy foods—and we're here to change that in our own small way.
> **C.** To nourish the world.

Option C it is. This is a short, big-thinking, and inspiring Purpose that will energize employees and attract customers. And no matter what types of food Stan may sell in the future, this Purpose can still stand.

Now try coming up with an alternate Purpose for Stan:

_____

_____

2. Shair

Shair's Vision: In the previous section, we changed Shair's original Vision from a long description of its offerings to "***Bringing people closer to the magic of entertainment.***"

Shair's Purpose: What is the *why* behind the *what* of Shair's Vision? Select the one you think works best:

> **A.** Connecting people to the Hollywood films they love.
> **B.** Empowering relationships.
> **C.** 'Cause people love movies!

Because the Shair application is all about connecting people, Option B—"***Empowering relationships***"—is a great Purpose for Shair. It aligns well with the company's Vision: "***Bringing people closer to the magic of entertainment.***"

Got a different idea for Shair's Purpose? Write it here:

_____

_____

3. Northeastern Data

Northeastern's Vision: Last time, we said that "***Protecting what matters***" was a better vision for this data-storage company than "*To make all our employees independently wealthy,*" since the former attracts customers and employees, not just employees.

Northeastern's Purpose: What is the *why* behind the *what* of Northeastern's Vision? Select the one you think works best:

> **A.** Protecting what matters.
> **B.** Protecting our customers from pesky system crashes.
> **C.** Protecting our company from financial collapse.

Even though option A is also Northeastern's Vision, it doubles well as a Purpose, just like Zappos's "*Delivering Happiness.*"

However, that's certainly not the only way Northeastern could go with its Purpose. See if you can come up with an alternative:

_____

_____

 # DOC'S PRESCRIPTION: CREATE YOUR PURPOSE

Now let's move on to the Purpose of *your* company. We'll assess whether your current Purpose excites your employees and motivates them to put passion into their efforts. Without this Purpose and its complementary Vision—the focus, the North Star—it will be nearly impossible for a great company Culture to arise. Now it's time to start thinking about your own Purpose. First write *why* your company does what it does:

_____

_____

Now write down *what the why* does to benefit the customer.

_____

_____

Write your current Purpose on the lines below. Again, this may be part of your current mission statement.

_____

_____

_____

How many words is it? _____

Do most of your employees know it?

☐ Yes   ☐ No

Is it clear, or is it confusing? How so?

_____

Is it memorable and repeatable?

☐ Yes   ☐ No

Does it accurately describe the *why* behind what your company does? How so?

_____

_____

Does this Purpose limit your future in any way? If so, how?

_____

_____

Does it inspire passion in employees, and show them that they're working for something bigger than themselves and the company? How so?

_____

_____

What do you think is right about it?

_____

_____

What do you think is wrong about it?

_____

_____

Your New Purpose

Now that you've done some thinking about your company's Purpose, use the lines below to jot down some thoughts on *why* your company does what it does. Imagine your company making the world a better place. Imagine going green. Imagine empowering and inspiring your employees and your customers. Imagine helping everyone reach their potential. Imagine doing or making something that benefits us all. Don't worry about keeping it short or focused right now—just get all your ideas down.

Here are a few ideas to get you started:

- Do you create a way for people to communicate?
- Do you give people a tool for learning, implementing, creating, or discovering?
- Do you give people a product that empowers them?
- Do you give people something to rally behind? (Think of TOMS shoes, whose Purpose is to provide shoes to children in need for every pair of shoes they sell.)

_____

_____

_____

_____

_____

Take the brainstorm above, and pick out the strongest idea or ideas. Write them below in a way that you think will benefit and attract employees and customers:

_____

_____

_____

Now distill that idea into one sentence that conveys your Purpose:

_____

_____

Can you get it down to six words or less without losing anything? Give it a try:

_____

If you're not happy with the Purpose you've arrived at, go back to your brainstorm and think about other reasons *why* your company does what it does. Before long, you'll come up with a Purpose that will inspire everyone in the company to get on board and give their all.

THE PURPOSE CHECKLIST

Hopefully you've been able to settle on a great new Purpose for your company, or have tweaked your old Purpose to really empower your employees and inspire loyalty in your customers. Before we move on, run through this checklist to make sure your Purpose meets all the criteria.

Our new Purpose . . .

- ☐ is clear
- ☐ is memorable
- ☐ is repeatable
- ☐ explains the meaning behind what we do
- ☐ creates passion in our employees
- ☐ extends beyond the walls of our company
- ☐ attracts customers and makes them loyal

Assuming your Purpose met all these requirements, write it again below, along with your Vision. Again, these are the two vital first steps you're taking toward a great company Culture.

Our Vision:

_____

Our Purpose:

_____

As we saw in our look at Google, Apple, and Zappos, many companies integrate Vision and Purpose into one statement. Do your Vision and Purpose lend themselves to this presentation? Give it a try here:

_____

_____

Can everyone still remember and repeat the Vision and Purpose statement? Is it still clear?

IMPLEMENTING YOUR NEW VISION AND PURPOSE

Congratulations! You have a clear, memorable, and repeatable Vision and Purpose that will attract customers and employees alike. Purpose plus Vision don't just equal the power of two: Combined, the effects are exponential for your employees and your customers. But you can't just write them down and leave them! A wonderful Vision and Purpose are useless unless people know about them, remember them, and focus on them.

You can't be like one company I worked with, where not one employee could come up with the Vision and Purpose on the spot, even though I was offering an iPad to anyone who did (and the Vision and Purpose had been created just six months earlier!).

Your Vision and Purpose have to become part of the company's DNA. Everyone—from the frontline to the executive suite—needs to remember *what* they're doing and *why* they're doing it. These two statements should act as a channel for the thoughts, actions, decisions, innovations, reinventions, and creativity that arise in your company. Think of your Vision and Purpose as the "clothesline" that employees can clip their direction and creativity onto.

Let's look at a few ways you can help implement your Vision and Purpose:

- Put the company's Vision and Purpose on everyone's **mouse pad.**
- Hand out **posters.** Place them throughout the hallways, in the elevators, around the lunchroom, in the reception area, and on bathroom walls. You want everyone to see the company's Vision and Purpose everywhere!
- Highlight the Vision and Purpose in the **company newsletter** and on the **intranet.**
- Organize **contests** around the Vision and Purpose.
- **Broadcast successes** by company employees that are tied to the Vision and Purpose.
- Create a **logo or tagline** that expresses your Vision and Purpose.

Now think for a moment about your company. Will any or all of the above ideas work for you? Are there other high-visibility ways you can reinforce the Vision and Purpose in your organization?

Name one or two ways you could do so that are not listed above:

1. _____

2. _____

Now consider which of these methods will have the most impact in your organization. I want you to write down your top three, and commit to implementing them over the next three months.

Implementation method #1:

_____

Implementation method #2:

_____

Implementation method #3:

_____

Your new Vision and Purpose, if consistently focused on by everyone in your company, will take you far—especially when fueled by the right Business Model, as we'll see in the next section.

3
BUSINESS MODEL

This is what will fuel us.

Objective:

To create or update your Business Model to support your Vision and Purpose and fuel your Culture, making sure it's aligned with the Information Age and with the wants, needs, and demands of your employees and customers.

Now that you've completed the Vision and Purpose sections of this workbook, you've created the first two key aspects of your company's structure. It is this structure that, if soundly built, will allow a great company Culture to thrive and perpetuate itself.

As you move through the remaining three structures of the Culture, keep in mind that these are all like building blocks, and each one you work on should be in alignment with all that came before. So, as you examine the Business Model that will fuel your company and Culture, it's important to ensure that it fully aligns with your Vision and Purpose. Above all, be sure that everything you create or transform passes the test of attracting employees and customers.

In a nutshell, a Business Model is the **plan implemented by a company to generate revenue and make a profit from operations.**

By making the Business Model one of the five key structures of the Culture, are we saying that making money should be your primary concern? No—as we saw in the previous sections, the profit a company makes doesn't directly motivate customers or employees, but it could, if it were aligned to their wants, needs, and demands. Making money is fundamental to keeping the business growing and the Culture strong, but it can't just be what's best for the company anymore.

If a business is not able to financially sustain its Culture and employees, layoffs will occur. After that, people see the writing on the wall and leave voluntarily. And it's pretty tough to keep up morale and sustain a great Culture when employees are fighting to keep their jobs, are scared, or are leaving. When things go downhill, employees adopt an attitude of being out only for themselves, team spirit suffers, and the same problems are delivered to customers.

BUSINESS MODELS: A FEW EXAMPLES

It's likely that you already have a Business Model up and running, but the goal of this section is to get you to think about how you can add to it, update it, or replace it so that it supports the Vision and Purpose, is aligned with the Information Age, meets the wants, needs, and demands of the customers and employees, and allows the Culture to thrive.

To open up your thinking about your own Business Model, let's look at a few types that have brought other companies success.

The Freemium Model. Wikipedia defines *freemium* as "a business model by which a product or service . . . is provided free of charge but a premium is charged for advanced features, functionality or virtual goods." People get to try out a product for free with an option to purchase or upgrade. It's like giving everyone a free sample and allowing them to decide if they want more. What's not to like?

The Platform Model. In this model, a company develops a scaffold or stage, as it were, on which individuals and large communities can sell their products. Amazon and eBay are great examples of platform Business Models. They capture almost all of what the Information Age has to offer, including cooperation from, and engagement with, employees and customers alike. These models allow employees to be part of something big, which also allows customers to be not only buyers but also sellers, and eventually those sellers can become buyers, too. Theoretically, when it's done correctly, you can double your employee "sellers" and customer "buyers" by creating a platform Business Model.

The Bricks-and-Clicks Model. Even companies with a physical store may not be able to compete in the future without an online presence. That's why a lot of enterprises have shifted to a bricks-and-clicks Business Model that basically lets them keep their physical store or business but also expand it exponentially by accommodating customers who place orders online.

WHAT MAKES A GREAT BUSINESS MODEL?

These are just a few examples to get you thinking about your own Business Model. The possibilities for the Business Model you can establish in your company are nearly endless, but there are a few key things to keep in mind.

1. Start by defining your market. Defining your market is paramount in creating your Business Model. Who are you trying to attract? Don't forget that the Internet and the Information Age have opened up new business opportunities and possibilities for you. Have you rescaled your Business Model to capture all of it? Remember, you don't have to be everything to everyone, but you don't want to limit your market either.

2. Treat people as an opportunity, not an expense. People want and deserve to be treated like they matter. Unfortunately, many companies' Business Models don't take people into account because they're too focused on making a profit. These companies are company-centric, and in today's Information Age, companies need to be employee- and customer-centric.

In your Business Model, you need to engage your employees and treat them like they matter. If you do that correctly, they will return the favor and treat the company the same way. They will become more engaged, creative, and efficient. But if you treat your employees poorly—even if your Business Model meets the wants, needs, and demands of your customers—you're bound to fail.

Likewise, the wants, needs, and demands of customers must factor into your Business Model. Many companies fail here, too. For example, I have spoken with many call-center employees who tell me that in most cases management considers phone conversations with customers to have little value. The calls are seen as an expense, and managers attempt to save money at every step. Employees are told to make calls as short as possible, and told to say no, no matter the request. Remember, your employees are your company's greatest asset—treat them that way.

Does saving these few dollars provide long-term value? No. This attitude costs the company, making it harder to add or retain customers. Creating a relationship with potentially lifelong customers is one of the most important things your Business Model should deliver or support.

3. Evolve or dissolve. In a Darwinian economic environment, unfit organizations—those that do not adapt to fit new circumstances—do not survive. According to "Business Model Warfare," a 2003 white paper written by Langdon Morris, "the average life span of an S&P 500 company has steadily decreased from more than 50 years to fewer than 25 years today." The message is clear: EVOLVE OR DISSOLVE! The wants, needs, and demands of your employees and customers are constantly changing, and your Business Model has to reflect those changes.

4. Scale to the Information Age. The Information Age has opened up all sorts of new avenues to sell a service, product, or knowledge. If the Internet plays no part in your Business Model, you're probably in trouble. But not everyone realizes how important this can be.

Many people have told me their company has not even come close to expanding its Business Model to capture everything there is to capture. These businesses haven't changed or adopted the Internet as their ally. In fact, some of them haven't even created a website! It's the way of doing business now and in the future, and such companies need to catch up mighty fast or risk falling behind competitors who are speeding along the Information Highway.

LegalZoom is a great example of such a company. Not only has the company used the incredible capacity of the Internet to reach customers in need of legal assistance, it has also met the needs and wants of customers by providing them with high-quality and easily accessible information on common legal concerns at an affordable price.

5. Don't miss out on key growth opportunities. Does your Business Model allow for new sectors that can drive your core business, or does it just keep you doing the same old thing? Any business that becomes successful attracts competition, which means the company has to keep ahead of the others by reinventing itself or opening up new aspects of its business.

Are there new opportunities aligned with your core business that you are not exploring? Are you leaving money on the table by limiting your offerings? One way to update your Business Model to capture new growth opportunities is to expand and maximize your offerings to reach new customers or grow the relationships you already have. If you're a law firm that works mainly with corporate customers, could you expand the existing relationships with clients and scale into taking care of their personal legal matters as well? This could be a fantastic adjacent business unit. Or, if you're a limousine company and have more customers than your fleet can handle, could you partner with another transportation company to meet those needs?

Are You Holding Your Customers Hostage?

I recently spoke to a friend who had been with her phone carrier for years and spent upwards of $150 a month. She wanted a new iPhone, but her provider didn't carry it. So she paid $200 to end her contract and went with a new carrier. Although the old company got her $200, it lost out on thousands of future dollars from her—and from the friends, relatives, and coworkers she recounted her distasteful experience to.

In the old days, many companies held customers hostage like this—think of record and book clubs that were hard to opt out of. Today's customers, however, want to be free to make choices, and thanks to technology, they have more choices then ever before. Yet, many companies still try to force customers into a contract—phone carriers and gyms are two common examples.

Holding customers hostage isn't a sustainable Business Model in the twenty-first century. Like another inadvisable Business Model—the hard up-sell—it will anger customers and frustrate employees.

Does your company hold customers hostage in any way? If so, explain here:

_____

_____

Is there a way to give your customers freedom without impacting your profit? Write your ideas here:

_____

_____

Another way to find growth opportunities is to specialize your offerings. For example, I met one dentist whose main work could have been simply filling cavities and doing cleanings. But he decided to focus on the cosmetic side of the business. His work is so sought-after that he opened up a school and lab next to his practice that teaches other dentists the science and art of cosmetic dentistry, and he has professionals flying in from across the country. Choosing a specialization has provided him with various businesses and a bounty of opportunities and possibilities that he would never have received if he had simply stayed a "regular" dentist.

6. Keep the wording simple. Some people believe that you should list the specific ways that you will offer your products, service, or knowledge, but that will only limit opportunities and possibilities in the future. As technology changes, you will need to keep up with the changes. So just as your Vision should be big enough to allow new opportunities for your company, a well-chosen Business Model will also be complementary to your success and will help fuel it.

PRACTICE

To help you get a feel for how companies can successfully update their Business Models, let's go back to our three example companies—Stan's Fruit Stand, Shair, and Northeastern Data.

1. Stan's Fruit Stand

Stan's established a new Vision and Purpose statement of "***Providing the finest-quality fresh organic fruits and vegetables to help nourish the world.***" Now, Stan is eager to adapt his Business Model so that the company can fulfill this Vision and Purpose in a bigger way. (Remember—this is all part of the structure that allows a great company Culture to flourish.)

Of the options below, which do you think is the best way for Stan to update his Business Model?

> **A.** Specialize in apples.
> **B.** Develop an affiliate program that encourages more local or specialized growers to sell through Stan's Fruit Stand.
> **C.** Buy buildings for two new locations.

Out of the choices above, option **B** is the best option. Moving toward an affiliate program could be a great way for Stan to cement his relationships with his vendors; offer a wider, fresher selection to his customers; and capture more of the market. This would be a move toward a Platform Model. Of course, we talked about how specialization could be a way to enhance the Business Model, but for Stan, option **A** would mean abandoning 90 percent of his offerings and focusing on a product that he can't make much more profit on, even if it's his specialty. Option **C** doesn't work too well because it does nothing to address how the company will grow into those new locations.

Do you have a different idea for how Stan could update his Business Model to better fuel the company? If so, write it here:

_____

_____

2. Shair

In the last section, we saw that Shair—the movie and entertainment app company—now has a Vision and Purpose statement of *"Bringing people closer to the magic of entertainment by empowering relationships."* To keep their Culture growing, Shair needs to update its business model; right now they're just selling a few 99¢ apps and selling a small amount of space to advertisers. Of the options below, which do you think is the best way for Shair to improve its Business Model?

> **A.** Start increasing staff levels through aggressive hiring.
> **B.** Up its app prices to $4.99 and start running twice the ads on its apps.
> **C.** Create a Platform that curates and distributes independently developed apps to all electronic devices.

Option **A** may artificially grow the company, but more people without more profit will be a detriment to the Culture in the long run. Option **B**—charging more and showing users more ads—will do little to improve the company's standing with employees or customers. But if Shair were to go with **C**—a Platform Model—and allow developers to create their own apps, it could focus on providing a great platform and distribution system for these developers' creativity. The company may also find itself freed from pressure to be solely responsible for creating apps, by allowing the world to help develop them. The change will likely invigorate Shair and push the company to live out its Purpose—*"Empowering Relationships"*—by fostering new connections between app creators and the users of the world.

Got an idea for another route Shair could take its Business Model? If so, write it here:

_____

_____

3. Northeastern Data

Northeastern Data has established a dual Vision/Purpose of *"Protecting What Matters."* Of these options, what's the best update Northeastern could give its Business Model?

> **A.** Focus on Mac users and drop their Windows-compatible products.
> **B.** Provide a Freemium Business Model.
> **C.** Start selling flash drives.

Option **A** isn't a great idea because it cuts out a huge piece of the market without adding benefit to the remaining piece. Option **C** isn't the best way to change the Business Model, although they certainly could sell flash drives if they wanted to. But plenty of other people sell them, and this small add-on won't give them that much added scale, and it doesn't take advantage of all the possibilities and opportunities offered by the Information Age.

Option **B** is the best of these choices because it allows Northeastern Data's customers to try out a basic version of their service for free. This would allow the customer to check out the product's ease of use and reliability. Once customers see what it can do, and hopefully are amazed, they will want more. They'll upgrade to a paid version—and in the meantime, you are creating a relationship with your Freemium customer. It's a win-win.

(P.S.—With Freemium offerings, you'd better make sure your product, service, or knowledge is top-notch. If it's not, very few will like your Freemium, and even fewer will become paying customers.)

Do you have an idea for another way they could update their Business Model?

_____

_____

DOC'S PRESCRIPTION: UPDATE YOUR BUSINESS MODEL

Let's take a closer look at your current Business Model. First, describe it briefly here:

_____

_____

Is it scaled to the Information Age?

Have you scaled your Business Model to the Information Age? Let's go through a quick checklist to find out how close you are. Does your company . . .

- ☐ have a robust website?
- ☐ offer self-serve ordering, without the customer having to talk to a salesperson?
- ☐ share free, helpful information with customers through its website?
- ☐ have some social media presence?
- ☐ ensure that its online presence aligns fully with its Vision and Purpose?
- ☐ equip employees with technology that enhances their work?
- ☐ meet the wants, needs, and demands of customers?

How'd you do? Were you missing any? If so, which ones?

_____

_____

Now think about whether you can incorporate any of these ideas into your current Business Model:

- The Platform Model
- The Freemium Model
- The Bricks-and-Clicks Model
- Specialization
- Adjacent business units
- Partner or affiliate program

Can you implement any of these in your Business Model? How do you plan to do so?

_____

_____

_____

_____

Can you think of any other ways your company can capitalize on the Information Age? If so, explain here:

_____

_____

_____

_____

Does it limit growth opportunities and possibilities?

Remember, the Information Age has changed everything and has also changed some of your customers' wants, needs, and demands. Is your current Business Model big enough to not limit these future opportunities and possibilities?

☐ Yes ☐ No

If no, how will you expand its scope?

_____

_____

_____

_____

Does this Business Model overlook important growth opportunities?

☐ Yes ☐ No

If no, what measures did you decide to take to change this? Sum them up here:

_____

_____

_____

_____

Could specializing your offerings provide your company with opportunities for growth?

☐ Yes   ☐ No

If yes, describe what this specialization would look like:

_____

_____

_____

_____

Does your Business Model meet the wants, needs, and demands of customers and employees?

Are all aspects of this Business Model in alignment with the needs and wants of your customers?

☐ Yes   ☐ No

If no, how will you change your Business Model to better suit these needs, wants and demands?

_____

_____

_____

_____

Does this Business Model contradict the needs and wants of employees in any way?

☐ Yes ☐ No

If yes, how do you plan to change this?

_____

_____

_____

_____

Any other changes needed?

After reviewing the examples of other Business Models in this section, have you identified any other ways you think your Business Model needs to change?

☐ Yes ☐ No

If yes, explain how you'll make these changes here:

_____

_____

_____

_____

Finally, check to see whether your Business Model fully supports your Vision and Purpose. Does it?

☐ Yes ☐ No

By now, you should have a good idea of how you might want to update your Business Model. Review your responses to the prompts above and list the changes you plan to make:

_____

_____

_____

_____

Now see if you can describe your new Business Model in a short but compelling way:

_____

Congratulations! You now have a Business Model that's in alignment with your Vision and Purpose, that supports the needs and wants of your customers and employees, and that will fuel the growth of your company and the creation of a great company Culture.

Before we move on to finding out how you can WOW your customers with unique offerings, recap the three building blocks you've established so far.

Our Vision:

_____

Our Purpose:

_____

Our Business Model:

_____

4
UNIQUE / WOW FACTORS

This is what makes us stand out.

Objective:

To establish the Unique/WOW Factors of your offerings.
These are what make you special, unique, and different from the rest;
your WOW Factor is a Unique Factor that elicits a positive emotion.
They allow you to stand out from the rest.

Imagine that a new restaurant opens in your neighborhood. You decide to try it, and head over with the family on a Friday night. You're seated by a friendly host and as soon as the waiter has taken your order to the kitchen, he returns with several bowls of piping hot gourmet macaroni and cheese.

"But we didn't order this," you say.

"Oh, I know—our chef makes the best macaroni on the planet. The mac 'n' cheese is on the house! Every one of our guests gets a bowl—no charge!"

As your family digs into the delicious macaroni, a feeling of goodwill comes over you. Assuming the meal that follows is as good as your complimentary starter, you'll be eager to tell friends and family about your new find—and eager to go back yourself.

This restaurant's free macaroni is an example of what I call a "Unique/WOW Factor." A Unique factor is something that sets you apart from all your competitors, while a WOW Factor ups the game by eliciting a positive emotion.

Virtually all businesses are about selling a product, service, or knowledge. The product, service, or knowledge, however, is only part of the total package. It is the Unique/WOW Factors that attract customers. If chosen properly, they will retain customers for life.

Two main kinds of Unique/WOW Factors apply to most companies and organizations:

1. **What** you sell (product, service or knowledge).
2. **How** you sell it (delivery) should be part of everything you do "in" your company and it should reflect everything that comes "out" of your company. It is what makes you Unique.

We all have opportunities to create Unique/WOW Factors around what we sell and how we sell it or do it. And companies can have many Unique/WOW Factors; they just all need to align with the Vision, Purpose, and Business Model.

Companies that sell things that are widely available at other companies and companies in the service industry should focus on *how* they sell (delivery), since *what* they sell isn't necessarily that Unique or WOW. At Zappos, many of the products can be found somewhere else, so the Unique/WOW Factors focused on how they sold it:

- Free shipping both ways
- A 365-day return policy
- 24/7 friendly customer service
- Signature white boxes that signaled to everyone: "This is a Zappos's shipment!"

Over time, the public will get to know you by your Unique/WOW Factors, and this will encourage customers to tell other people about you, creating word-of-mouth. Your Unique/WOW Factors will be your one-of-a-kind calling cards. They'll tell everyone, including customers and employees, what you are about. You'll be "buffing out" all your customers by allowing them to get what you offer differently than they do from anyone else. They'll see that you are taking extra steps to create a fantastic experience for them.

For example, See's Candies is known for quality without compromise. Have you ever gotten a bad chocolate from See's? One that was discolored, tasted different, was broken, or less than perfect? Probably not. This commitment to quality, consistency, and perfection in *what* they sell is a crucial Unique/WOW Factor for See's Candies. But they are also Unique/WOW on *how* they sell—just look at their beautiful packaging and stores!

Walmart, unlike See's, doesn't have a much of a Unique/WOW Factor for *what* it sells, as you can get most of the products they sell just about anywhere. Instead, they chose a Unique/WOW Factor that applies only to *how* they sell it: everyone knows that Walmart equals value and low prices; that's what makes their stores Unique.

Unique/WOW Factors can be just about anything you do to stand out from the rest in your industry, or the world for that matter. Here's a list of some of the Unique/WOW Factors that have helped companies expand and prosper:

- Market disruptor
- Experience with an Emotional Connection

- Best service and experience
- Being totally unique
- Providing service
- Being different

When choosing your Unique/WOW Factors, you really want to make them part of your company's DNA. If you choose service, for example, everything you do must align with service as the Unique/WOW Factor, and that starts with delivering great service to your employees. They'll reciprocate by delivering great service to your customers. If service is emphasized within your company, it will be strong enough to reach those outside.

PRACTICE

To get a little more comfortable with the concept of Unique/WOW Factors, let's take a look at our three companies and see how they can separate themselves from the crowd, either in **what** they're selling or **how** they're selling it.

1. Stan's Fruit Stand

You'll remember that Stan's Fruit Stand has set out with this Vision and Purpose: *"Providing the finest-quality fresh organic fruits and vegetables to help nourish the world."* What are some ways the company could differentiate itself from other fruit stands? Pick the best option from these:

> **A.** Provide signature fruits and vegetables not found in other stores.
> **B.** Offer a free Big Mac coupon with every purchase over $15.
> **C.** Offer a wide selection of organic produce.

The options for ways to stand apart from the crowd are nearly endless, but of these three, **A** is Stan's best bet. When people see his unique variety of signature fruits and vegetables that they can't get anywhere else, they'll keep coming back for more, especially when they compare Stan's to an ordinary fruit stand—there will be no comparison. Option **B** isn't a great choice because it's not in line with the company's Vision of *providing the finest-quality fresh organic fruits and vegetables* and its Purpose of *nourishing the world.* C isn't the best because it isn't very unique or much of a WOW—tons of places offer a wide selection of organic produce.

What's another way Stan's Fruit Stand could make itself Unique/WOW? We'll start you off with one:

1. All packaging and bags at Stan's are compostable.

2. _____

_____

2. Shair

Now let's move on to Shair, the entertainment company with the Vision and Purpose of "***Bringing people closer to the magic of entertainment by empowering relationships.***" It has recently converted to a Platform Model, where it allows developers to create apps that it then distributes to all types of mobile devices. Choose one good Unique/WOW Factor from these actions that Shair might take:

> **A.** Make all its apps free, with no ads.
> **B.** Have a strict one-strike policy for developers—if one of their apps tanks, Shair no longer works with them.
> **C.** Provide live chat to connect app users and app developers.

Option **A** might attract customers, but it also would likely undermine Shair's Business Model. With little or no revenue model in place, how will it incentivize developers, fuel the Culture, and keep growing? Option **B** might give Shair a reputation for uncompromising quality control, but will it attract developers (who, in this model, are almost like employees)? Not so much. Option **C** is the best of these three; this Unique/WOW Factor is aligned with the company's Vision and Purpose, and it also empowers relationships between the individuals who make the apps and the customers who buy the apps. This will ensure the success of the company, as those relationships created in the live chat function will help the developers create what the customers want, need, and demand far into the future.

What are some other Unique/WOW Factors Shair could establish?

1. Provide live chats for focused areas of entertainment—theater, film, arts, sports, and so on.

2. _____

_____

3. Northeastern Data

Northeastern Data has developed a multi-platform data storage system that can hold all of its users' important files, whether large or small, personal or professional. This is all part of its dual Purpose/Vision of *"Protecting What Matters."* Of these three options, what's the best Unique/WOW factor for Northeastern?

> **A.** Offer a thirty-day free trial.
> **B.** Promote a function that automatically deletes all customer files that haven't been opened in seven days.
> **C.** Offer a quick and easy one-step storage solution for all electronic devices (similar to Amazon's one-click checkout).

Of these, **C** is the most unique and the most in line with Northeastern's Vision/Purpose. It also allows an easy one-step solution for all storage on all devices. Option **A**—a thirty-day free trial—may indeed be a good idea, but plenty of other similar services offer that. And option **B** is all about clearing out files—the opposite of the secure, all-encompassing storage Northeastern is building a reputation for.

Have any ideas for other Unique/WOW Factors Northeastern could implement?

1. Provide a dashboard of all the customer's storage devices and items contained in them. This could tell customers, "No more sifting through different files, accounts, or locations to see what you have stored."

2. _____
   _____

DOC'S PRESCRIPTION: CREATE YOUR UNIQUE/WOW FACTORS

You may have some Unique/WOW Factors already. If you do, write them below. (If not, don't worry—most companies don't. We'll help you think up some in just a moment.)

Your Current Unique/WOW Factors:

1. _____

   _____

2. _____

   _____

3. _____

   _____

Think about any Unique/WOW Factors you listed above. Are they . . .

- ☐ truly unique?
- ☐ able to WOW?
- ☐ known to your customers and employees?
- ☐ likely to create word-of-mouth?
- ☐ consistent with your Vision and Purpose?
- ☐ consistent with your Business Model?

Do they . . .

- ☐ separate you from the rest?
- ☐ create a positive emotional reaction?
- ☐ attract employees?
- ☐ attract customers?

If all boxes are checked, you likely have a strong Unique/WOW Factor that you'll want to hold on to. But if any came up lacking, you may want to think about updating or discarding them.

Your New Unique/WOW Factors

Now let's work on developing some new Unique/WOW Factors. Imagine that you or a close family member is about to do business with your own company. What would you want to experience? What would really knock your socks off? How can you best "Buff them out"? Brainstorm on the lines below:

_____

_____

_____

_____

What can you do that others don't do?

_____

_____

What can you do that others *can't* do?

_____

_____

List three potential new Unique/WOW Factors for your business:

1. _____

_____

2. _____

_____

3. _____

_____

Are all three in line with your Vision, Purpose, and Business Model? If any aren't, explain here:

_____

_____

_____

Which one do you think is strongest?

_____

Do these Unique/WOW Factors attract employees who want to deliver them?

☐ Yes   ☐ No

If yes, how so? If no, why not?

_____

_____

_____

Do these Unique/WOW Factors attract customers who want to buy your offerings, and will they prompt word-of-mouth?

☐ Yes   ☐ No

If yes, how so? If no, why not?

_____

_____

_____

Now compile your original Unique/WOW Factors that made the cut, and add any new ones you came up with here:

1. _____

_____

2. _____

_____

3. _____

_____

IMPLEMENTING YOUR UNIQUE/WOW FACTORS

You've now established some great Unique/WOW Factors, but you're not done yet. Follow these three steps to implement and regularly update them:

1. **Let your employees experience them.** If you "bake in" the Unique/WOW Factors and extend them to your employees, they'll reciprocate by providing or delivering them to your customers.
2. **Be Consistent.** Your Unique/WOW Factors won't do a lot of good unless they are consistently provided or delivered. You can expect word-of-mouth to help spread the news, but only if the Unique/WOW Factors are provided or delivered consistently.
3. **Update them as needed.** Unique/WOW Factors, over time, don't always stay unique. If you're not paying attention, they can go the way of the rotary phone before you even notice. So consistently evaluate your Unique/WOW Factors to ensure that they're still Unique and WOW.

Our Vision:

_____

Our Purpose:

_____

Our Business Model:

_____

Our Unique/WOW Factors:

1. _____

2. _____

3. _____

4. _____

5
VALUES

This is what we care about.

Objective:

To create or update your company's Values, so you can tell the world what you value and let them know who you are.

We're now on the fifth key structure in creating your company's Culture: its Values. If you create Values that are aligned with all the other aspects—especially Vision and Purpose—you are going to attract folks who are going to create the Culture or bring it to life.

Values are what we hold close to us and what we consider important. They are, quite simply, what we Value.

Most people know it's important that a company establish and live by a set of core Values, but too many don't know how to pull this off. Leaders at one company I visited, for instance, showed me their list of ten core Values. Yet after reading them, I couldn't quite figure out what all of the points meant. When I asked about one Value in particular, the CEO reread it and said, "In other words, it means . . ." Values should not have to be explained. They should be clearly written, stated, or declared. Core Values are a part of the blueprint of who we are, what we do, and how we do it. But if your Values aren't understandable, how will they attract employees and how will your employees live by them?

Establishing a strong set of core Values will allow your Culture to manage itself. Once you attract those who value what your company Values, you don't have to worry about making sure they will uphold those Values. That's a main reason why they joined your team. It's just the way things go: Those who are in alignment with your Values will join the company and will attract others like themselves. Those who aren't in alignment with your Values will leave.

Make sure to create values that will support and drive behavior that will not only empower employees but will also be aligned with what your company offers and what it delivers. For instance, if you've set your sights on having same-day delivery of your offerings, you wouldn't want to create this Value: "We take our time." Even though it would empower your employees to take their time, it wouldn't support your company's focus on providing same-day delivery.

As you come up with your Values, you can use one word or a combination of words. You can also come up with a core Value word and then add words to modify it: if one of your Values is "Excellence," you could expand it to "Delivering Excellence" or "Delivering Excellence to our Customers"—whatever you think will best help your company create your offerings and support their delivery.

Your Values can be employee focused, customer focused, or vendor focused and can be creation focused or delivery focused. Any combination you come up with is fine. That's the cool thing about Values—you can create anything you want! You can also have as many as you feel are necessary (within reason), whether it's four or ten.

Perhaps you already have a few. If you do, our goal will be to help you evaluate them and update them as needed. And if you haven't yet established any Values, we'll help get you started. First, let's look at some of the most important characteristics of powerful Values that will help sustain your Culture.

1. Your Values should be unique to your company's offerings or the experience you deliver. This doesn't mean you have to dream up Values that no other company has ever used. But it does mean that you need to tailor your Values to your company. Again, they need to be in full alignment with everything you've built so far: your Vision, Purpose, Business Model, and Unique/WOW Factors.

For example, the Values of firefighters would be much different from those of a nursery school. The firefighters' Vision/Purpose might be to "Save Lives," and their Values might relate to teamwork, caring, courage, community, to mention just a few.

Meanwhile, the nursery school staff might embrace a Vision/Purpose of "Nurturing Lives." The concepts the nursery school might build its Values around could include patience, love, kindness, and compassion.

2. Your Values should be realistic. Whatever we choose as our Values— whether as individuals or as part of a country, religion, team, or company—we must be able to live by them.

For instance, say you value getting things done, and you state that Value as "Always giving 110 percent." Nice try, but "Always giving 110 percent" is an impossible goal. Think about it: Can you imagine always giving 110 percent? You would burn out on day one.

3. Everyone in your organization should be living up to your Values. Just as values are part of one's individual character, they are also part of the character of a company. You can state your personal Values, but you really let others know about your Values by what you do and how you act. Values, when chosen wisely, over time will shape behavior to empower your employees and will support and help drive your offerings and delivery, thus empowering the Culture, company, and its positive growth.

Do leaders in your company live and breathe your Values on an everyday basis? Whether they do or not, people can see it.

Enron is a great example of a company that failed here. The company's stated four Core Values were Respect, Communication, Excellence, and Integrity. The firm even had all sorts of objects that proclaimed its Core Values, including paperweights. But there was a huge disconnect between the company's words and its actions. It fostered a cutthroat Culture that encouraged employees to turn on each other, and its leaders, of course, cooked the books to hide heavy losses. Enron could have been a fine company had its leaders lived up to their stated Core Values, but they didn't. That was the company's downfall.

Oprah, on the other hand, and all the brands she represents show how following through on your Values can show everyone she's truly about what she says she is. Her name alone evokes a positive response. Oprah's consistent message—from her interviews and television talk show to the articles in her namesake magazine—is all about self-empowerment and living up to one's potential. And she lives that Value in her widespread philanthropic endeavors, such as funding a girls' school in Africa. If we are living up to the core Values that we declare, people perceive us as a shining light.

The Unfortunate Result of No Values

Does a company *have* to establish core Values? If it wants to build a strong Culture it does! Here's what happens if you fail to establish Values that define what you and everyone at the company are all about:

- There's a disconnect between employees and management.
- Few will stay on schedule or meet deadlines.
- Employees and customers will be treated poorly.
- Poor management skills will be coupled with poor leadership.
- Employees will lack the empowerment to help the company.

Don't let this happen to you!

4. Your Values should empower your biggest asset: employees. Employees are your company's biggest asset, and the Values you create for your company should empower them, not only within your business but also in the employees' personal lives.

Above all, remember that the Values you choose should allow your employees to reach their own potential, personally as well as professionally. When the employees are empowered in their own lives, they will raise the company with them.

PRACTICE

To get a little more comfortable with the concept of Values, let's look back at our three example companies.

1. Stan's Fruit Stand

Stan's Vision and Purpose is *"Providing the finest-quality fresh organic fruits and vegetables to help nourish the world."* Of the choices below, which is the best example of a great Value? One of Stan's Fruit Stand's Values could be:

> **A.** "Committed to freshness and the finest quality."
> **B.** "We embrace frozen foods."
> **C.** "We meet company needs at all costs."

Hopefully it's clear that **A** would be the best choice, as it is right in alignment with a good chunk of Stan's Vision and Purpose. Option **B** might make the company happy, by giving their product a longer shelf life, but it's out of alignment with what they've set out to do. And option **C** is all about the company—not the employees or customers—which is a big no-no in the Information Age.

What could be some other core Values for Stan's Fruit Stand?

1. _____

2. _____

2. Shair

Shair's Vision and Purpose is *"Bringing people closer to the magic of entertainment by empowering relationships."* What's one core Value this mobile app distributor could set for itself? One of Shair's Values could be:

> **A.** "Embracing creative genius."
> **B.** "Love."
> **C.** "We will get perfect ratings from every one of our customers, every time."

Option **A** is the best choice here; for a tech company, "Embracing creative genius" is an appropriate Value that will inspire and attract employees and customers alike, helping to create a strong creative Culture—not to mention all the future offerings it can come up with by listening to the wants, needs, and demands of customers, and all the apps that the developers can create to put on the Shair platform. Option **B**, on the other hand, is too vague, while **C** is something no company could realistically live up to. When Shair's employees faced an inevitable customer complaint, they would feel frustrated.

List two other potential Values for Shair here:

1. _____

2. _____

3. Northeastern Data

Northeastern Data's Vision and Purpose is *"**Protecting What Matters**."* Of the choices below, which is a strong Value that Northeastern could establish for itself?

One of Northeastern Data's Values could be:

> **A.** "Security."
> **B.** "Fashion-consciousness."
> **C.** "Taking it easy."

Again option **A** is the best of these options. Security is very much aligned with Northeastern's Vision and Purpose. If the company lives up to this Value, it will promote redundant systems that will ensure security should one system fail. Its customers will automatically think of the concept of security when they put high-value data in the company's hands. Option **B**, on the other hand, has little value to offer either customers or employees, and option **C**, "Taking it easy," may attract some nice, relaxed employees, but taking it easy certainly isn't in alignment with "Protecting What Matters," especially when it comes to securing someone's valuable data.

DOC'S PRESCRIPTION: CREATE YOUR VALUES

Before we get started on working on your company's Values, I want to make an important point: Everyone should be involved in this process. If the company's leaders meet alone and come up with a new set of Values, when they share them with everyone else, those left out will likely feel resentful and uninvolved. You don't want to say to employees, "Hey, these are the Values you're going to live by!" If I told you what values you should live by in your own house, you would probably kick me out!

Instead, bring everyone in on this process in some way. Even if the company is too large to include everyone in the initial meetings, run the proposed Values by everyone and ask for input.

Let's start this process by listing any Values you may currently have.

Current Values

1. _____
2. _____
3. _____
4. _____
5. _____
6. _____
7. _____
8. _____
9. _____
10. _____

Think about the Values you listed above. Do they . . .

☐ accurately represent what everyone at the company Values?

☐ support your Vision and Purpose?

☐ help drive your Business Model and the products, services, and knowledge you offer (and the delivery of these offerings)?
☐ support your Unique/WOW Factors?
☐ attract and empower employees?
☐ attract customers?

Are they . . .

☐ something you can realistically live up to?
☐ clearly articulated?

If all boxes are checked, you likely have a strong Value that you'll want to hold on to. But if any came up lacking, you may want to think about updating or discarding them.

Which ones will you be keeping?

1. _____

2. _____

3. _____

Which will you be discarding?

1. _____

Why?

_____

2. _____

Why?

_____

3. _____

Why?

_____

Now I want you to have a brainstorm. List all the words you can think of that represent what you want your company to be all about. Don't worry about forming distinct Values right now; just write what comes to your head. Bring everybody in on this discussion—not just the executive team or managers. The more *everyone* participates, the better buy-in you'll get down the road.

The Values Brainstorm

_____

_____

_____

_____

_____

_____

Did you come up with some good ideas? I hope so. Now I'd like you to look back over your ideas and pull out a set of Values that you think are the best representatives of what your company truly stands for and cares about. Remember, it's okay if you only have three or four.

1. _____

2. _____

3. _____

4. _____

5. _____

6. _____

7. _____

8. _____

9. _____

10. _____

How are they looking? Are you close? Before you officially establish any of these, run them through our Values checklist:

Do they . . .

- ☐ accurately represent what everyone at the company Values?
- ☐ support your Vision and Purpose?
- ☐ help drive your Business Model and the products, services, and knowledge you offer (and the delivery of those offerings)?
- ☐ support your Unique/WOW Factors?
- ☐ attract and empower employees?
- ☐ attract customers?

Are they . . .

- ☐ something you can realistically live up to?
- ☐ clearly articulated?

Now you can write all the Values that made the cut on the next page, along with all the other pieces of the structure you've built so far!

Our Vision:

_____

Our Purpose:

_____

Our Business Model:

_____

Our Unique/WOW Factors:

1. _____

2. _____

3. _____

4. _____

Our Values (you can choose any number of Values):

1. _____

2. _____

3. _____

4. _____

5. _____

6. _____

7. _____

8. _____

9. _____

10. _____

6
CULTURE

This is what is and what could be.

Objective:

To examine and optimize the Culture of your company—the living, breathing, thinking, and creative sum of all the beings who work there.

In the previous five sections, we've covered the five key structures that make up the foundation or framework of your company's Culture—Vision, Purpose, Business Model, Unique/WOW Factors, and Values. I hope that you've now had meaningful discussions about each of these and have established a strong framework using these five interrelated structures.

So what's the next step? Well, we just need to bring these structures to life!

The previous five structures are merely words, yet they are special. They have meaning for not only *what* you do, *why* you will be doing it, and what you Value; they will also continue to fuel your Culture and make you Unique/WOW.

In the five sections that follow this one, we'll discuss five more important aspects of Culture, but rather than structural elements, these will be more like interior design elements, which will turn your house into a home. Each one will help make your business a great place to work, to create, and to deliver experiences that connect you and your people emotionally to customers—and them to you!

But before we move on to those aspects, we're going to stop and create ways to breathe life into the structure you've built so far: the Culture itself.

One of the greatest Cultures in the world is that of the United States. Our founding documents—the Declaration of Independence and the Constitution—had all the structures we have gone over in the first five sections: A Vision (*what* we do), a Purpose (*why* we do it), a Business Model (that fuels the country), Unique/WOW Factors (that attract people from around the globe), and our Values. Our Founding Fathers skillfully established a Culture of freedom, liberty, and choice. The structure of that Culture allowed the creation of the living, breathing, thinking, and creative sum of all Americans. Acting as one in respect to the structure of this Culture, Americans have accomplished great feats.

If you create a similarly great Culture within your company, your group, team, or organization will thrive. If you surround your employees with all of the positive attributes that a great Culture can offer, the foundation is set for everyone to be happy and empowered, proud to be a part of the company and eager for it to thrive.

Culture is what you do, why you do it, and how you do it, along with the language, beliefs, thoughts, decisions, and actions of your organization. Culture holds everything together; it is the glue, and without it the organization would revert to separate individuals out only for themselves.

A great corporate Culture is an asset to any business. Studies have revealed that companies with a Culture aligned with the key aspects of its business and its goals routinely outperform their competitors at 200 percent or even more. Here's a sobering statistic: 50 percent of S&P companies in the 1950s were not around in 1970. And 50 percent of companies in 1970 were gone by the 1990s. Basically, the average lifespan has shrunk from fifty years to twenty-five years—and it's still shrinking. What happened? The Cultures that didn't foster creativity or innovation didn't evolve with the times. And they sure didn't attract customers—or, most likely, employees. Thus, companies are dying at a much faster rate than before. I'm sure that if we, as a civilization, were to see human lifespans cut in half, we would immediately look into the "Why?" behind the change. In the same way, we have to understand why companies are failing faster and more often—and the solution starts with Culture. When you see that your company isn't moving in the right direction, it's time to transform your Culture.

It's the people within the Culture that will bring the Vision, Purpose, Business Model, Unique WOW/Factors, and Values to life with language, beliefs, thoughts, decisions, and actions that are in alignment with all of the above. Culture, if created, implemented, and sustained correctly, not only helps attract employees and customers and strengthens their allegiance to the business, but it also helps with the bottom line.

KEYS TO A GREAT CULTURE

Let's now take a look at several of the keys to a great Culture. Keep in mind that every company has a different Culture, and that's as it should be. This isn't a "how-to" book for you to replicate what some other company did. You can use other great company Cultures as models, but be sure to make yours unique: Culture is something that only the members of **each individual organization** can create, because it's what they themselves think, value, and do.

Also understand that a Culture doesn't pop up instantly. You need to make a plan, create it, and follow it. And there will be much less resistance to change when the Culture has been created by the people who have to live it—so, as with all the other aspects we've talked about, try to include as many members of your team as possible in the discussion of where your Culture is at and where you want it to go.

With those things in mind, here are some of the fundamental parts of company Culture.

1. Vision and Purpose

As you know, Vision and Purpose are primary among the key structures that support any Culture. You may have heard management say that you need to "be on the bus or off the bus," meaning that everyone on the team should be going in the same direction, together. But *what* is your bus doing and *where* is it going? And *why*? Does everyone know the destination? And is there a good reason to aim for it?

Write your Vision and Purpose here:

_____

_____

Does your Culture—or will it—align with the Vision and Purpose? If you can think of any way in which it doesn't, explain here:

_____

_____

2. Common Language

All cultures have a common language. But over time, without constant work to keep the language aligned with the company's Vision, Purpose, Business Model, Unique/WOW Factors, and Values, that language will be diluted.

Leaders need to be constantly aware of what is said in the company, and of how it's said. At times, language can move from being positive and uplifting and in alignment with the five key structures to being negative and out of alignment. Rather than giving people lists of rules to follow or constantly telling them what not to do, encourage communication of the structures of the Culture in a way that creates an aligned language and can-do spirit.

How would you characterize the common language in your company?

_____

_____

Does your common language bring the five structures of your Culture to life?

_____

_____

6: CULTURE 59

3. Beliefs

All great Cultures have beliefs. What beliefs characterize your Culture? Does your Culture rely on employees who can figure things out and take the company to the Next Level? Does it empower and serve employees and customers? Or does it stress profits at any cost, even if that kills the goose that lays the golden egg? Customers find out the answer to that question by looking at what your company does.

It's likely that your company's beliefs are revealed in its Values and in what you create and deliver. What are two of your organization's beliefs? List them below, and on the next line reflect on whether the Culture and your company's actions reflect this belief.

Belief #1:

_____

Is it reflected in the Culture?

_____

_____

Belief #2:

_____

Is it reflected in the Culture?

_____

_____

Do your beliefs bring the five structures of your Culture to life?

_____

_____

4. Attitude

The attitude of a Culture is the "vibe" you get from everyone. Is it positive or negative? Do the employees of your company think the Culture is great or are they wondering if it would be better to work somewhere else?

List a few words or phrases that define your Culture's attitude or "vibe":

_____

_____

Does this attitude or "vibe" line up with the structure you created in the last five sections—including the Vision, Purpose, Business Model, Unique/WOW Factors, and Values? If you answered no to any, explain how you might shift the attitude to align better with the structures of your Culture:

_____

_____

_____

_____

Now make a new list of words or phrases that define the attitude or vibe of your desired Culture:

_____

_____

Does the attitude or "vibe" in your company bring the five structures of your Culture to life?

_____

_____

5. Work Ethic

Work ethic is about how members of the Culture work. Do they spend long hours alone in their cubicles, or do they take time to communicate with their coworkers and create better relationships? Do they arrive early in the morning? Stay late at night? Whatever the work ethic of your company, it should balance growth and creativity. The point by now is familiar: We need to treat people like they matter.

Countries differ in their work habits, such as hours and vacations. For instance, in Spain, workers take a siesta around midday, then go back to work and stay later into the evening than Americans do. Companies vary in the same way.

One of the companies I am involved with has a task-oriented culture that seems to be aligned with the wants and needs of today's employees; as a result, the business is doing rather well. The whole team gets together every Monday and maps out the work to be done for the week. Then they all go their separate ways to meet the goals. The company attracts employees who like to work alone without distractions. I talked to one worker to get his feedback on the Culture. "I like it," he said, "because I go to sleep working on my laptop and wake up with it. Most of the time, if I have to get ready and travel to work, it's a disruption."

What is the work ethic of your company Culture? Describe below how your employees work. Long hours? Short hours? At home? Strictly in the office? By doing this and making it transparent, you will attract employees who are aligned with your work ethic.

_____

_____

_____

Does this work ethic component align with the needs, wants, and desires of your employees? If not, what changes do you need to make? Write your thoughts below, and perhaps even have a few discussions with others to inform your answer.

_____

_____

_____

Does your company's work ethic bring the five structures of your Culture to life and support the creativity and delivery of what you offer?

_____

_____

6. Relationships with Coworkers

Most people need and want good relationships with coworkers. But perhaps your Culture doesn't emphasize this aspect. If so, that's fine. It's perfectly fine if you prefer—like some Silicon Valley companies—to hire gunslingers who will likely be around only temporarily. It's nevertheless important that you are transparent about this aspect of the company Culture, so you don't end up attracting people looking for close relationships with their colleagues. They will be disappointed and will soon leave.

How does your Culture approach relationships among coworkers?

_____

_____

Is this approach in line with your desired Culture? If not, what can you do to increase that alignment?

_____

_____

_____

_____

Do your relationships with coworkers allow the five structures of your Culture to come to life?

_____

_____

To create and maintain a great Culture, focus on the keys: Vision, Purpose, Business Model, Unique/WOW Factors, and Values, and then a common language, beliefs, attitude or "vibe," work ethic, and building relationships with coworkers. At times you might need to focus more on one element than another. But that's to be expected. Creating a culture is an organic process because you're working with the living, breathing employees who bring it to life.

> ### Does our CEO's personality have to match the Culture?
>
> Culture either has to come from the top or be green-lighted by leaders; otherwise, it will not be sustainable. People always follow the actions of those in charge.
>
> But not every CEO has a personality that matches the company's desired Culture. If your CEO is quiet, cranky, or curt, for instance, it might not matter as far as the overall Culture is concerned. All the CEO has to do is approve, green-light, and encourage a Culture with a more relaxed and positive vibe.

DOC'S PRESCRIPTION: EXAMINE YOUR CULTURE

In the following pages, we're going to take a closer look at some of the specific elements of your Culture and challenge you to reflect on how they enhance your team's performance—or how their absence is holding you back. If certain areas of your Culture are great—perfect. Keep it that way and focus instead on the areas that need to change. Just remember that Culture is all-encompassing—it should help support everything else. It should bring all the other pieces to light and put them into practice.

1. Is your Culture exciting?

Dull is dead. The language, attitude, and "vibe" of your company are important parts of the Culture, helping your employees feel a sense of excitement, inspiration, direction, purpose, and passion in a big way. Plan to put a little excitement in the lives of everyone at work, whether it's through a simple potluck, a field trip, an acknowledgment and recognition program, or a birthday celebration for each employee. It's a minimal investment that leads to energized employees. And that excitement will spill over to your customers as well.

List three current ways you have put excitement into your Culture here:

1. _____

2. _____

3. _____

What are three other ways you could make your employees' work lives a little more exciting? Remember, they don't have to be lavish or expensive.

1. _____

2. _____

3. _____

2. Do you have a Culture of salutations?

A greeting may seem like a little thing, but over time, salutations can take on huge significance in your Culture. A smile and a genuine "How are you?" or "Nice to see you" goes miles in anyone's book. Would you really want to work at a place where no one smiles or acknowledges your existence?

As an invited guest to many businesses, I have often been completely ignored. Literally, no one greeted me when I arrived. Even though I could see 30 employees within 50 feet, no one looked up, or if they did, they looked away. Boy, would I love to work there—not!

Do your company's salutations support the "vibe" you want in your company?

_____

_____

On a scale of 1 to 10, how do you think your employees do at greeting guests and each other?
_____

How about you? What's your salutation score? _____

If either score was below 8, take some time to think through how you can encourage salutations that enhance your Culture. Write your ideas here:

_____

_____

_____

_____

3. Do you have a Culture of traditions?

Traditions help unify a group and give everyone a sense of belonging. Look at the Culture of any foreign country and you'll see what I mean. The traditions of a country, for example, are aligned with the overall structure of that country's Culture. Acknowledging and celebrating traditions within your company will help keep the traditions of your company strong and provide a sense of being part of something special.

> ### Is Your Culture Being Passed Down to the Next Generation?
>
> A great Culture requires a conscious effort to ensure that it's transmitted from generation to generation. If your Culture is geared toward the needs, wants, and desires of the workforce of twenty years ago, it's going to be badly out of date. The majority of your employees today are likely Gen Y's and Millennials, and they have a very different set of priorities than the baby boomers.
>
> It's increasingly important therefore to make sure the Culture is passed on to the next generation and that it evolves with the new wants, needs, and demands of the employees and customers, while keeping your company's DNA intact.

Do you have any traditions that are currently part of your Culture, whether they're just fun inventions or a meaningful part of the company's history? If so, list them below:

_____

_____

_____

_____

Do your traditions support and align with the five key structures of your Culture?

☐ Yes   ☐ No

If you had few or no traditions, brainstorm below about a few new ones you could put in place:

_____

_____

_____

_____

4. Do you have a Culture of creation and innovation?

Does your Culture provide freedom, opportunity, and the liberty to create and reinvent? Does your staff have the freedom to add value to what you make? Are your Vision and Purpose blueprints for creativity? How many times have your employees heard the words, "No," "Don't," or "You can't"?

Many companies fail to stay current with the wants, needs, and demands of the employee and customer. Teams and departments often just keep doing what they're doing; they don't stop to innovate. It's not on purpose. It's just that most of the time our priorities get messed up. People get so immersed working *in* the Business that they neglect working *on* the business.

Sometimes we need to take a **time-out** to reassess our priorities and identify what is truly important. Are we in alignment with the Information Age and the wants, needs, and demands of employees and customers? Are your creation and innovation aligned with the Vision, Purpose, and Values of the company? Are your Business Model and your Unique/WOW Factors up to date? Even more crucial, is our Vision and Purpose up to date and still attracting employees and customers? Once we've ascertained these things, we can make it a point in the future to "check yourself, before you wreck yourself . . . and your business."

Do you feel your company culture encourages creation and innovation? Explain why or why not.

_____

_____

_____

_____

If you found your Culture lacking in this area, what are some actions everyone can take to encourage more creation, reinvention, and innovation? One of these may be a **time-out**, as discussed above.

_____

_____

_____

_____

Does your creation and innovation support the five key structures of your Culture?

_____

_____

5. Do you have a Culture of leadership?

Does your leadership help create your Culture and help put that Culture into the company's DNA? Does your company have great leaders who have the opportunity—and regard it as their duty—to help others become leaders and promote the Culture? Does your company mentor employees so that they can reach their potential? Or do you have suffocating managers who tell grown-up people what to do and how to do it? Yikes!

Great leadership empowers your employees to take their lives to the Next Level; they will then take the company to the Next Level as well! The next section goes into leadership in detail, so we'll examine this aspect closer there.

6. Do you have a Culture of planning?

In underdeveloped countries with poor transportation planning, carts, donkeys, bikes, motorcycles, buses, and cars all compete for the same lanes. Result: gridlock. Does that sound like your company? Or is there a blueprint for all to follow? Does your company have a well-thought-out plan to grow, or do decision makers shoot from the hip?

How strong is your company's planning, on a scale of 1 to 10? _____

If you scored below an 8, brainstorm some ideas on how you can build the planning aspect of your Culture:

_____

_____

_____

_____

7. Do you have a Culture of employees?

Does everyone need to have "exactly" the same attitude and share the "exact" same values that frame your Culture? No, of course not, because we are all different and unique. But they shouldn't be too far off base, either. Look at your friends; most likely, they share the same general attitudes and Values you do, though some may be more dynamic and engaging than others.

Would you say that most people at your company share the same Values? Explain below:

_____

_____

_____

_____

If you feel you're lacking in this area, what are some ways you could work this into your hiring process?

_____

_____

_____

_____

8. What's the mind-set behind your Culture?

Does the mind-set of your Culture align with the outcome you desire? If not, you can transform your employees' mind-set over time, beginning with articulating Values.

What makes up a positive mind-set? In my experience, executives and employees all come up with the same list of Values:

- Getting things done
- Figuring things out
- Taking it to the Next Level
- "Spin it & Win it" (This is a phrase I use to mean that anytime we are faced with a challenge, we turn it into a positive opportunity or lesson.)
- The bigger the challenge, the more fun it is

Think about your company's mind-set and describe it here:

_____

_____

What about it is good? What needs to change?

_____

_____

_____

_____

Now list two ways you can help convey the desired mind-set to employees. (To get you started, I'll give you an example: After I gave a talk at the Adidas headquarters, the company embroidered Adidas hats with the saying "Spin it & Win it" for all their employees to wear.)

1. _____

2. _____

NOW, DOES EVERYONE KNOW WHAT YOUR CULTURE IS?

Once you have chosen the ways you want to bring your Culture to life, it's crucial to make sure everyone knows what it's about. Everyone needs to walk the walk and talk the talk. You can have a great structure, but if no one lives it or follows it, it's dead.

For example, does your company consider e-mailing on weekends a standard practice, or do you, in the interest of balance, e-mail only if absolutely necessary? All employees should know the answer right away.

Some people will like one type of Culture, others will be drawn to a different type. It's better to be transparent about yours; otherwise you'll end up with one of two things—a disgruntled employee who stays or a disgruntled employee who leaves. Either way, you lose.

Now that we've examined your Culture in depth, we're going to move on to five important aspects of company Culture. Again, these are going to be like the furnishings that fill out the structure you've created thus far, and they will bring the structures of your Culture to life. The first aspect we'll talk about is Leadership, which plays a huge role in empowering employees and keeping the structural foundation of the Culture in place, now and in the future.

7
LEADERSHIP

This is empowering and passing the torch.

Objective:

To examine the leadership in your organization, which is crucial to leading both the employees and the Culture that will be key to the organization's success.

In the first five sections, we covered the five key structures that will act as the foundation of your Culture and will drive and support it. Now that we've done that—and examined the Culture itself in the previous section—we're going to look at five key aspects of the Culture: the interior design elements that enhance or create results of the structure you've built so far.

First up is a big one: Leadership, which plays a huge role in empowering employees, driving the Culture, and keeping the structural foundation of the Culture in place and growing stronger.

Leadership can do three things: Lead the company up, lead it down, or lead it sideways.

You can articulate the great structures of a Culture, but if the Leadership does not pollinate it throughout the company—including the vocabulary, processes, and procedures that will drive, support, and bring your Culture to life—it will go nowhere. They can bring the Culture to life or leave it dead in its tracks, depending on what they do and how they do it. Without proper Leadership, the structure and the Culture itself will be only words.

So take a good look around at the Leadership of your company. Are leaders "baking in" the structures of the Culture you have created? Are they using vocabulary that's in alignment with the Culture on a daily basis? Are they helping to develop processes and procedures that ensure that the structures of the Culture are becoming part of your company's DNA—in other words "how everyone does things," now and in the future?

Remember, we have all been through some tough times in the economic downturn for over a decade, and we now are standing tough and want to be treated like we matter. We have more choice in whom we work for than ever before. The wants, needs, and demands of the employee

> "People don't really care what you know, unless they know you care."
> —Tom Mendoza, Vice Chairman at NetApp

must be treated like they matter, because in the Information Age, they sure do matter. If an employer acts otherwise, news travels fast.

With the structure of the Culture in place, especially the Vision, Purpose, and Values, we no longer have to tell employees what to do. They know what needs to be done, so there's no need to manage them like we did in the Industrial Age. We just need to lead them and ensure that they all know and understand the structure of the Culture. If they do, they will make sure it is implemented.

We've all heard the expression "It's not what you say, but how you say it," and this statement could not be truer. If we want to bring the Culture to life, the Leadership needs to act as a guide, and make sure that the message delivered is in alignment with the Information Age and the wants, needs, and demands of the employees.

DO YOU MANAGE PEOPLE, OR DO YOU LEAD PEOPLE?

First, it's important to recognize a crucial distinction between managing and leading. Leadership comes from within management, yet many times no one within management is truly leading—only managing. And if you want to engage the employees, managing them is the wrong way to go. There is a difference between leadership and management. As the saying goes: **lead people and manage things** (like numbers and processes).

Think about Stan, the owner and primary leader within Stan's Fruit Stand. Stan needs to manage things like his inventory, his cash on hand, his overhead, his hiring process, and his growth plan. But he needs to *lead* the people who make up the company and the Culture. If Alice, one of his top employees, reports to work and finds that Stan is trying to manage her just like he would a balance sheet, she'll grow unhappy very quickly, and the Culture and the business will suffer.

In a nutshell:

Leaders don't tell people what to do; they let them know what needs to be done and help them if necessary.

In your company, you want to be part of a chain of empowerment, not a chain of command. This leads to happy employees, which leads to happy customers, which develops into a happy business.

Managers have power *over* people. Leaders have power *with* people.

DO YOU CRITICIZE, OR DO YOU GIVE FEEDBACK?

Say that Rick, CEO of Northeastern Data, gets a lackluster report from Bryan, one of his employees. It's clear that Bryan didn't spend much time on it, and it was a couple of days late. Which of Rick's responses do you think will be most helpful in this situation?

> **A.** What the heck, Bryan? This is one of the worst pieces of work I've ever seen—worse than Samantha's even. Better step it up if you want to be around in six months.
> **B.** Great report, Bryan!
> **C.** Bryan, you've done great work for this company, but this report isn't quite up to your legendary standard. How do you think I can help you so that your next report showcases that great work you're famous for?

Clearly, option **C** is the winner. This compliments, praises, and approves of Bryan's work, and it allows him to receive help if he wants it. It is leadership like this—leadership that focuses on employees' greatness, not their shortcomings—that supports a great company Culture. (Meanwhile, option **B** is both dishonest and unhelpful, and option **A** would likely just cause resentment and fear.)

> **Shine light on what someone does right, and you'll see more of what you like.**

To help bring the positive spirit of option **C** back to your team, think of one positive word that you will use frequently over the next thirty days:

_____

Use this word liberally, and after thirty days, try a new one. You'll find the whole team will start using more positive words, and the vocabulary of the team will go to the Next Level.

TEAMS MIRROR MANAGEMENT

Just as customers mirror employees, employees mirror management. If you, the leader, break an employee's trust, they will mirror your action and lose trust in you as well. And if you have an employee who doesn't care about you, it's undoubtedly because you don't care about them.

Imagine that Susie, the leader of Shair's customer support team, is at the end of her rope with the people under her. Susie says, "The employees gossip all the time, and no one seems to care about the company." Given this mirroring principle, what do you think is the most plausible theory as to what's going on?

> **A.** Susie's team all decided at a happy hour that they no longer liked their manager.
> **B.** Susie has been too easy on her team, and they've decided to exploit this perceived weakness.
> **C.** Susie has herself shown little enthusiasm for the company and has been gossiping. The team has seen this and is mirroring her attitude.

Yes, option C is the most likely scenario. When leaders or managers are having problems with their team, they need to ask if the problems are a reflection of their own behavior. How can employees who are abused take care of customers any differently? The answer is *they can't*. But if leaders take care of the employees, their success will translate to the customers.

Keeping in mind that teams mirror management, what kind of traits would you like to see in your team?

_____

_____

_____

_____

Whatever you wrote down, make sure you are setting the stage for these traits in your own actions and behavior first.

THREE KEYS TO GREAT LEADERSHIP

A leader can raise the employees' expectations of themselves, reinforcing their abilities and getting them closer to their full potential. Leaders also embrace the positive, which allows them to be effective and inspirational role models. There are three important keys to becoming a successful leader: **self-improvement**, **communication**, and **relationships**.

Key #1: Self-improvement. Employees can match a leader's knowledge and capabilities, but it may be difficult for them to surpass them. So to keep the company advancing, a leader should be working on self-improvement, too.

When leaders take the initiative to better themselves, they can pass along their new knowledge and wisdom to the entire team. As we said before, teams mirror management, so to ensure your team is taking things to the Next Level, the leader has to take the first step.

Leaders must rely on their own self-improvement in order to keep the team moving forward. Figure out what you need to do to empower yourself, then, in turn, empower your team. Your team is a reflection of you, and you want that reflection to shine as bright as the sun.

What kinds of self-improvement do you think you need to do in order for the Culture to become the best, and for employees to reach their full potential?

_____

_____

_____

A Leadership Hall of Horrors

We all know stories of bad leaders, whether we personally experienced it or heard it from a friend. Here are the three types of bad leaders you'll see most often. These types all have one thing in common—they try to manage people rather than *lead* people.

The Ivory Tower Leader. This type thinks he's far better than the minions below him. He usually has a secluded office, perhaps even with an access key. His employees rarely see him, and he has no clue how they're feeling at any given time.

The Bullying Leader. The bullying leader may not physically harm you, but you may hear her say things like "If you don't do what I say, there will be consequences," or "It's my way or the highway." With a bully like this at the top, meetings function poorly, there's little collaboration, and people are generally miserable. In a nutshell, the Culture is severely compromised by bullying leaders.

The Lazy-Loaf Leader. Everyone on the team has a purpose, but the leader must set the tone and help execute the plan. The leader who doesn't is what I call a Lazy-Loaf leader. He knows what needs to be done, but doesn't do much about it. Like the others, this type of poor leader hurts the whole Culture.

Key #2: Communication. Proper communication is crucial to any organization. It can unite a team and help it accomplish great things, but a disconnect in communication can actually lead to the downfall of a company.

Unfortunately, fast-growing companies frequently experience problems in communication. As the firm grows, however, the voice of the leader becomes fainter, and employees can misinterpret it. Weekly executive meetings are an effective way to keep communication open and the Culture intact, but a little small talk can create big results. Great leaders ask their employees about family, life, goals, and interests. If leaders really care, employees understand that they are concerned not just about work, but about truly knowing them. That's what leaders do. Ask about spouses, children, and hobbies. Call employees by name. (Our names are the sweetest words we can hear!) In turn, employees will get to know their leader.

Here are a few tips to make your communication stronger as a leader:

- **Personalize communication.** Instead of "Nice job," try "Mary, I noticed that report you wrote. It was one of the most detailed and professional reports I have ever seen."
- **Use "we," "ours," and "us"** more than "me" or "I." Words like these emphasize a team spirit and indicate that we're all in this together.
- **Use employees' names.** Believe me, one's name sounds 10,000 times better than anything else.
- **Communicate promptly**—inside and outside the company—whether by e-mail, phone calls, or one-on-one chats.
- **Be interested.** People are flattered when you show them attention.
- **Listen** without distraction, and try to listen twice as much as you speak.

Make a list of the things you can do to better communicate with your team:

_____

_____

_____

Key #3: Relationships. If leaders need employees to care about the company, leaders must start by caring about their employees. Think of it as paying it forward. A relationship goes both ways; there has to be give-and-take. You help me and I'll help you. **I care about you and you care about me.**

We've all heard that employees don't quit their company, they quit their boss. Why? Usually because acknowledgment and recognition were nowhere to be had, so the employee feels there is no real purpose or reason for him or her to be there. Showing your gratitude to employees will not only fulfill their needs, it will demonstrate to others what kind of work earns accolades; it's another win-win. Taking a sincere and genuine interest in others creates rapport and builds leadership.

What can you be doing to help build great relationships with your employees?

_____

_____

_____

DOC'S PRESCRIPTION: EXAMINE YOUR LEADERSHIP

In the final pages of this section, we'll delve into your strengths as a leader and where you can improve. But to get you primed, run through this checklist. For each row, place a check in either the right or left column based on which statement you feel better reflects your leadership style. If you're in the column on the right, this is an area you need to work on.

The Leadership Checklist

☐ I take responsibility for my employees' growth.	☐ I see the employees' growth as their responsibility.
☐ I am generally a caring authority figure.	☐ People see me as distant and detached.
☐ I motivate employees through my own actions.	☐ I tend to give directions from the sidelines.
☐ I create leaders.	☐ I manage employees.
☐ I elevate employees' lives and that of their families.	☐ I have little impact on my employees' personal lives.
☐ I want leaders on my team.	☐ I want employees on my team.
☐ My vocabulary is consistently positive.	☐ I let negativity creep into my vocabulary on a regular basis.

Of the above items, which did you feel was your biggest strength?

_____

Your biggest weakness?

_____

What Kind of Leader Are You?

People no longer settle for the traditional boss–employee dynamic in which grown men and women are told what to do by an executive who tries to manage or boss them, rather than lead them. No more "powerful and powerless." No need to enter a workplace filled with orders, rules, and restrictions. No more being told what to do and when to do it. Those days are over.

Let's start your examination of your own leadership skills with this question: Who's the best leader or mentor you've met in your career?

_____

Briefly explain what made him or her such a great leader or mentor.

_____

_____

What do you think you can learn from this person?

_____

_____

Now, in the space below, write what you consider to be your best leadership skill. When I do this exercise with groups, I usually get a different answer from everyone. I'll give you a few sample skills to start off:

- Trustworthiness
- Takes ownership
- Listens
- Sincerity
- Caring

So what's your best skill?

_____

What do you think is your weakest area when it comes to leadership?

_____

Did you see yourself or at least part of yourself in the descriptions of Ivory Tower leaders, Bullying leaders, or Lazy-Loaf leaders?

☐ Yes ☐ No

If yes to any, how do you plan to counteract that tendency?

_____

_____

Would you say you tend to compliment more or criticize more?

☐ Compliment
☐ Criticize

Explain your choice. If you criticize more, what steps can you take to move toward complimenting?

_____

_____

_____

Do you thank the people you lead regularly?

☐ At least once a day
☐ Once every few days
☐ At least once a week
☐ Very rarely
☐ Never

If you checked either of the last two boxes, write one strategy to remind yourself to thank your employees more often. Maybe it's a pop-up reminder on your computer, or a short weekly meeting you institute where you can give thanks and show gratitude. What's your strategy?

_____

_____

_____

In the same vein, list two ideas for how you can focus on your employees' greatness below. What are some ways you can shine a light on what they're doing right?

1. _____

2. _____

Which of the three keys of leadership—**self-improvement, communication,** or **relationships**—do you think you're strongest in?

_____

Can you think of a way to capitalize on that strength and take it to the Next Level?

_____

_____

Which do you feel is your weakest point?

_____

What can you do to improve in this area?

_____

_____

Hopefully this section has helped you learn more about the Leadership at your company—and about your own skills in this area. It will be your job to lead the Culture, and set it up in a way so that all its parts are aligned. In the next chapter, we're going to discuss one of the leader's key allies in actually implementing and sustaining the Culture: the new Human Empowerment department.

8
HUMAN RESOURCES / HUMAN EMPOWERMENT

This is the group of champions.

Objective:

To transform your current Human Resources department into a Human Empowerment" department—one that will help empower employees and champion the Culture.

In the previous section, we explored the Leadership at your company, and looked at how the Leadership can and should be an integral part of your company's Culture and your employees' success. It is the job of leaders to *lead* the Culture and build it into the DNA of the organization.

But what happens once the supporting structures of the Culture are in place?

This is where Human Resources steps in. They are the ones that can champion the implementation of all aspects of the Culture and keep it growing stronger. Basically, they are the ones who do everything that has to do with empowering and engaging the employees—as long as it's in alignment with the Culture that we created!

In this section, we're going to look at how your HR team (or perhaps your HR person, if you're at a very small company) can take the baton from Leadership and ensure that all the structures of the Culture—Vision, Purpose, Business Model, Unique/WOW Factors, and Values—are being instilled in the Culture. We will also focus on creating empowered and engaged employees, so that the Culture remains strong—and growing stronger.

FROM HUMAN RESOURCES TO HUMAN EMPOWERMENT

HR does so much for the company and its employees, but much of it goes unrecognized. When I directed my chiropractic clinics, a disproportionately large segment of our patients were HR employees. Out of curiosity, I started asking them about their jobs, and I heard the same response many times: They were constantly caught up in "he said / she said" arguments that had escalated out of control. They were under a lot of stress and tension, and on top of that, many felt they had an undeserved bad rap.

It's true that, to many, HR has a negative connotation. If you get sent to HR, you think you're about to get fired, or get in trouble. It's like being sent to the principal's office.

But Human Resources is about giving *resources* to *humans*, and shouldn't that be a good thing? Absolutely! Shouldn't employees look toward HR as a place where they can receive support? Absolutely! Plenty of HR employees work hard at doing this, but often the negative connotation remains.

Since the very name HR gets in the way of accurate perceptions, why not begin by changing the name? Everyone in a company should view HR more like what it is and can be: a combination of a loving, caring, empowering department that helps take employees to the Next Level. Changing the title to **Human Empowerment**—HE—gives the department a fresh start.

The new name will help employees focus their thoughts, decisions, and actions on empowerment, just as having a clear Vision and Purpose aligns the company and moves everyone in the same direction.

HE can be the single biggest champion of your company's Culture. After all, they are the ones who have the relationships with and trust of the employees. What if your new HE department was always asking employees if they needed anything or if there was anything they could do to help? That would be taking a proactive—rather than reactive—stance toward building relationships.

> **HE can have the biggest impact on the Culture, through the empowerment and engagement it delivers to employees!**

Allow your HE department to empower and engage your human assets and your Culture. If you do so, you'll find that HE can really help out with the Culture and brand. If the company's Culture is shining on the inside, the brand that people see outside will shine as well.

The following pages reveal seven ways you can start transforming your HR department into an HE department. HE can and should go way past the point of hiring the employees. Once on-boarding starts, there are a lot of ways the HE Department can empower and engage employees to reach their full potential, and when that's done right, the company will reach its full potential too! As you read these, remember that all your HE programs should be focused to empower and engage your employees while being aligned with the overall Culture structure of your company.

1. Start a Coaching Program

As I learned in my clinics, HR professionals face a ton of stressful situations. One great way to defuse these before they need HR intervention is to create a coaching program.

Consider assigning someone within your HE team as the Coach, and letting employees know they can come to that person with thoughts and concerns—whether those concerns have to do with their professional lives or personal lives. As someone who's served as this kind of coach before, I know that most of what the coach has to do is simply listen. When the coach sits down with an open mind and open ears and lets the employee talk about any challenges they might have, over time the employee will often come to a solution to a challenge on his or her own!

The HE coach's Vision and Purpose will be to help employees reach their full potential. He or she will meet with all the employees individually and let them just talk and listen to them, get to know them as a person, and be available if they need to get things off their chest. This simple process will help resolve all sorts of problems before they escalate, and will result in better communication and better relationships (and, ultimately, a stronger Culture).

Do you have someone currently in your HR department who could serve as Coach? Or do you have the resources to hire someone to fill this role?

_____

_____

_____

2. Write a Positive Daily Blog

Another great way for HE to empower employees and implement the whole structure of the organization (Vision, Purpose, Values, etc.) is to start a blog that features daily motivational and inspirational messages. These can be delivered to all employees over the company intranet every day. Give your employees the opportunity to start their day reading something positive.

Do you currently have a positive company blog in your organization? If not, will you start one within the HE department?

___

___

___

Your organization can even sign up to TheCultureSecret.com to have your employees receive inspirational and motivational blog posts. (These are the same posts that were delivered to the employees at Zappos to help with a positive mindset and can-do attitude for the employees.)

3. Help Employees with Goal Setting

Consider having your HE department or coach set up a goal-setting program for employees. This will encourage them to communicate with HE, and feel more empowered and engaged. The HE staff or coach should let employees open up about their overall dreams in life and then help them find ways to make these dreams a reality. Again, this is often accomplished by simply listening!

Here's an important point, though: Make it clear that the HE department's goal-setting program is for personal goals, too, not just for work goals. If employees weren't doing well in their personal lives, setting professional goals wouldn't matter. And even if they were doing well in their personal lives, an emphasis on professional goals will be seen as just pushing them to do more work. Rather than empowering them, the professional-goals-only approach feels like the company is saying, "Set bigger goals at work, so you can work more and work harder . . . for us."

Experiencing wins in one's personal life allows for more empowerment overall; work gets better, too—because newly empowered employees improve all aspects of their life.

You also want to make sure the goals set by the employees are easily accomplished. Make them easy to win and hard to lose. If the employee experiences success in goal setting, it will be easier for them to go back to the process over and over—raising their own life up, step by step!

Do you think a goal-setting program will work at your company? If you already have one, does it offer support to employees personally, or is it strictly for professional goals?

___

___

___

4. Enhance Hiring Processes

One of HE's functions is, of course, to oversee the hiring of employees. As you move from HR to HE, make sure the team's hiring processes are in line with the structure and the Culture.

Fitting into the Culture is the very reason we pay so much attention to the people we accept for employment. Applicants can be as smart as a whip, but if they are difficult to deal with, they don't fit the Culture and should be dismissed. Standout team members who can't get along end up spoiling the Culture of the team.

The HE team can also consider replacing two-hour interviews with a fun and engaging group interview process. First, set up a meeting for all the candidates for a position. One HE has outlined the company's Vision, Purpose, and Values, set up interviews—three or five minutes apiece—for each candidate with three of your employees. Use a set of prearranged questions, and have your employees rate the candidates. This type of hiring technique isn't perfect for all positions, but it helps determine Culture fit, it involves, empowers, and engages employees, and streamlines the hiring process.

And the process shouldn't stop at hiring: it should involve taking care of employees long after they are hired. We spend so much time and effort on hiring—why should it all stop once an employee is on board? Nope, the "honeymoon" should never end at your company—keep showing the love.

Does your HE department currently look at Culture fit, and does it involve non-HE employees in the hiring process with the aim of empowering employees and engaging them once they are on the team? If not, what can your new HE department do to change this?

_____

_____

_____

5. Start a Company College or University

Consider developing an internal training department, a "college" or "university," that helps employees move to the Next Level. Your HE department can provide benefits in the form of such classes, which help employees develop personally as well as professionally.

For example, you can have history classes to pass along the background and traditions of your company, since history is a large part of any company Culture. How about Excel and word-processing classes to help them be better qualified? How about having a speed-reading class for personal empowerment? How about having an accounting class focused on budgeting and saving in the employees' personal lives?

As with the goal-setting program, there is no need to have all the classes focus on company matters; it's the people who count. When you empower your employees at a personal level, they will reciprocate and help move the company forward.

Does HE currently provide company history and empowering education to employees at your company? If not, can you create a company university to do so?

___

___

___

6. Deliver Fun!

Since the new HE department creates great relationships, those staff members can be responsible for seeing that everyone has fun. Breaking up the workday with fun times really helps improve the morale—almost as much as food does. Let's face it—we all like to have fun. So why does fun have to be "saved" for our off time?

Consider appointing an "ambassador of fun" within your HE department; this team member can organize children's and spouses' days and other events that promote unity among those who give their days to your company.

Celebrations are a great way to increase the fun at work, break the monotony of redundant tasks, increase communications, and solidify relationships. Your HE department can arrange ice cream socials, cookouts, potlucks, and employee, vendor, and customer appreciation days. Oh, and don't forget a "we don't need a reason" approach to delivering food to your employees. Food creates good morale as well as good communication and helps cement long-lasting relationships.

How often do you celebrate and have fun at your company? Can you have the new HE team increase the fun that will strengthen your Culture? If so, what kinds of celebrations or activities can you implement in your company to increase the fun?

___

___

___

7. Collaborate Regularly

As we've said, communication—or lack thereof—is often the biggest challenge in a company, especially one that's growing. Don't let your teams or departments get "siloed" into isolation.

An "all hands on deck" meeting organized by HE is a great way to get the company together, and if you don't have enough space to include everyone at the meeting, stream it live to the biggest rooms that will accommodate as many people as possible to hear the message. There should be a "group takeaway" from the meeting, a common affirmation that will support the common language within your Culture.

Do you currently have regular all-hands-on-deck meetings? If not, will you start? If you already have these meetings, are they optimized to increase communication and build a common language?

_____

_____

_____

DOC'S PRESCRIPTION: TAKE A CLOSER LOOK AT YOUR HUMAN EMPOWERMENT DEPARTMENT

You hopefully have some ideas percolating about how you can transform your HR team into a great HE team, so let's now take a closer look at how you're going to do this. Although positive signs can't counteract a negative Culture, if you are changing HR into HE or transforming your Culture to be more empowering and engaging, let the world know it, but start with your company! If everyone is aware that they are in transition, going from "what is" to "what will be," the new Culture will be adopted more easily.

Do your employees currently feel empowered and engaged by the HE Department?

_____

_____

What can your HE Department do to change its past negative HR connotation, if it has one?

_____

_____

_____

What is your HE Department currently doing right?

___

___

What is the biggest challenge you see in your current HE Department?

___

___

Teams and departments tend to become "siloed" over time. What steps can your HE department take to increase communication and adopt a common language between other parts of the organization? Would dedicated liaisons help?

___

___

___

What is the first step you're going to take to make this change a reality, whether it's one of the seven ways to transform your HR department into an HE department listed on page 83 or something else? Describe how you plan to implement it over the coming days and weeks.

___

___

___

Almost everything that makes up a company's Culture can and should be championed by the HE Department. If this is done correctly, HE will enhance positive feelings about working at your company—and you'll find that your customers benefit, too, as we'll see in the next section of this workbook.

9
CUSTOMERS AND CUSTOMER SERVICE

This is essential to the process.

Objective:

To enhance or transform your Customer Service so that it meets the wants, needs, and demands of Customers (because without them, there would be no company or Culture).

Every company owes its existence to its Customers. It is the Customers who come to us, so it is our duty, opportunity, and privilege to meet or surpass their wants, needs, and demands. It's important that we do everything in our power to make their day, week, month, or year—right? So why not serve *them*—that is what Customer Service is all about.

Regrettably, Customer Service has become wallpaper—something people talk about a lot without thinking about what serving the customer really means. For many companies, Customer Service has not caught up with the times. Customer Service used to take place in person, then it was over the phone, and now it relies on phone plus the Internet and various other devices. The personal connection that worked in the past is not as personal as it once was, and many companies haven't caught up with the Information Age in the way they provide true Customer Service.

Let's look at some ways Customer Service is delivered by many companies nowadays before we take a closer look at how you can enhance or transform the Customer Service you're giving to your own customers.

CUSTOMER SERVICE ISN'T "CUSTOMER, SERVE US"

Recently, I went to a fast food restaurant chain with my family during a long road trip. We got our order, and I noticed they'd forgotten to include my wife's tacos. But before I had a chance to alert the server to the problem, he was asking us if we would take an online customer-service survey, because he said, "it would really help" him.

"Maybe," I said, as we sat at the drive-through window, "but first could we get the rest of our order? You seem to have forgotten a few things . . ."

The server left for a moment and returned after a few minutes with part of the order that he'd forgotten and again asked me to complete the online survey. As we drove away, we discovered he had not only forgotten the rest of the order, but he'd given us the wrong tacos—the cheaper versions, to boot.

Why couldn't he have just given us what we ordered and paid for, instead of being focused on us taking a survey that would help him, even as he shorted us and gave us the wrong items? Why would a fast-food restaurant chain have its employees focus on a survey that serves the company instead of focusing on Customer Service—serving the customers, and giving them what they order? This company has turned Customer Service into "Customer, Serve Us." It's saying, "Pay us, and then we will ask you to do something for us." What's with that?

This is a perfect example of how self-centered many companies have become. They have become company-centric instead of being customer-centric. Sure, they want to collect customer-satisfaction data, but it's mainly for their own purposes; and it costs them a lot of customer satisfaction.

CUSTOMER SERVICE AS A "SAFETY NET"

Today, many companies use Customer Service as a safety net to address customers' problems, questions, or concerns after they've bought a product, service, or knowledge. They haven't created their offerings in a way that minimizes (or eliminates entirely) the need for Customer Service. But if you need great Customer Service to put out fires, it's often too late; some customers that go into or slip past the net are hard to win back. You shouldn't need to repair, fix, or improve your Customer Service if your offerings are top notch. Customer Service needs to be "baked in" to the product, service, or knowledge that your company offers. When your product, service, or knowledge is flawed or junk, and when Customer Service is just an add-on that takes place later, you turn the Customer Service department into the complaint department.

Customer Service is **making sure those complaints don't happen in the first place**. Companies do this by aligning their Customer Service with the wants, needs, and desires of their customers, and by weaving it into their offerings instead of leaving it to the end. (We'll talk more about the Experience in the last section of this workbook.)

Imagine that Northeastern Data has been experiencing more customer complaints than usual, and that company leadership has put together a team to see what they can do about it. Of the choices below, what do you think is this team's best course of action:

> **A.** Assess the company's offerings, and identify steps that can bring these offerings further into alignment with customers' needs, wants, and desires, as well as with the company's Vision/Purpose of *"Protecting What Matters."*
> **B.** Issue a blanket $100 coupon on future services to all current customers as a thank-you for doing business with the company.
> **C.** Develop a comprehensive questionnaire to ask why the unhappy customers are unhappy.

As you likely guessed, option **A** is the best here. This approach will fundamentally improve customer service, support the Culture, and help retain customers. Option **B**, on the other hand, is little but a Band-Aid, while option **C** basically asks the customer to do more work to help the company. If Northeastern data works at building great customer service into its offerings from the beginning, there's no need for the latter two approaches.

ARE YOU KEEPING YOUR CUSTOMERS, OR JUST ACQUIRING NEW ONES?

If our Customer Service enables us to reach and retain a positive emotional connection with our customers, we have the chance to keep them for a lifetime. Most companies have measured the cost of acquiring a new customer, but few, if any, have calculated the cost of retaining the customers they already have. I would argue that the scale is usually tipped in the wrong direction.

If we did everything we could to take care of the customers we have, that effort would pay for itself over and over again. Look at it this way: If an average customer spends $200 a year and the lifetime of buying is 50 years, that person will spend $10,000 if you keep them happy. If your initial customer acquisition cost was $50, you will receive $9,950 in gross revenue from just that one customer.

In addition, that **one customer's word-of-mouth over the years will have a snowball effect on your income.** Think of the revenue stream generated just by keeping this one customer happy. Then multiply that by the total number of your customers; you'll have all the business you can handle. And this is what you call turning a *sales business* into a *reorder business*.

Conversely, when a company loses an existing customer as fast as it acquires a new one, income and the company will never grow. It's as though you have a hole in your bucket: whatever you put in will drain out at the same rate, and the bucket will never fill. More often than not, unsatisfied customers tell their friends (and a bad experience typically travels a lot farther and faster than good news)—that, of course, drives the customer acquisition costs up. As it becomes increasingly difficult to acquire customers, the company's income plummets.

Imagine that Shair's CEO attends a conference session about Customer Service and comes back jazzed about the idea, but without any concrete ideas on what to change. Of the choices below, which direction do you think is best for him to move in?

> A. Plan a massive campaign to have users of Shair's applications leave positive reviews for these apps, in an effort to show potential customers how happy current users are.
> B. Offer a deal that gives new customers a coupon for a free app when they buy their first app.
> C. Focus attention on Shair's offerings, asking themselves, "How can we make our apps and our platform more intuitive, rewarding, and empowering to our customers?"

Option **A** isn't the best—again, you're asking your current customers to expend effort just so you can get more customers. That's company-centric, not customer-centric. And option **B** isn't best either; this will draw in a few new people, but does that matter if your current customer base is thinning out just as fast as you add new buyers? Option **C**, on the other hand, puts the focus on improving the experience for existing and potential customers alike. As Shair's apps and platform improve, customers will naturally start telling more people about the company.

GIVE CUSTOMERS CERTAINTY

As you read further, you'll see that customers may say they want things like value, service, low price, high quality, selection, guarantees, and so on, but one thing they all agree on is that they want "certainty." We need to be consistent with our product, service, knowledge, and delivery. (And, once again, this all starts with providing your employees with the certainty that you've got their best interests—as people, not pawns—at the top of your mind.)

Imagine that you like a certain type of catsup and are willing to pay more for the brand. You love the flavor, taste, and consistency of that particular catsup. One day you run out of your favorite catsup and go to the store to buy another bottle. But when you open it, it's runny and tastes a bit off. So you throw it away and go back to the store and buy another bottle and everything is again fine. A few weeks later, you run out of catsup again and go get another bottle, but this time it's too thick and again tastes "off." With this inconsistency, you soon lose your love for the brand and stop buying it altogether. As customers, we want consistency, and if we don't get it, we start looking to buy something else.

In addition to being certain that the product, service, or knowledge they're getting from you is consistent, customers also **want to be certain that you'll go the extra mile for them**, even when it would be easier for you or your employee to say no to a request or skimp on a cost. Say a restaurant serves a decent plate of food for $12, with a cost of $2. What if it upped the amount it spent on ingredients to $3?

I had a friend who did just that, and after a while, customers were lining up out the door of his establishment—without the cost of advertising. My friend was now making money hand over fist, and the customers not only came, they returned.

Imagine that a guy walks up to Stan's Fruit Stand and asks the woman behind the counter whether they have rambutan fruits. The employee knows that Stan's has never carried this exotic fruit, and that it's so expensive (and the demand for it so low) that the company wouldn't make much of a profit if it did. What do you think is the best response she could give the customer, of the options below?

> **A.** "Nah, you're going to have a heck of a time finding that in this part of town."
> **B.** "No, but we have some lychees, which are pretty similar to rambutans."
> **C.** "We don't right now, but let me see what we can do. If we can get some, would you still be interested?"

If Stan has trained all his employees to give customers the certainty that their wants, needs, and desires will be met, then the answer this customer will get is something like C. Option **A** will result in a frustrated customer; option **B** contains good information and shows that the employee is knowledgeable, but if the response stops there, the customer is likely to still be disappointed. Option C, however, will show this customer that he matters. Stan's Fruit Stand may not make much profit on stocking a few rambutans for him, but the customer will almost certainly make up for this by shopping at Stan's more often—and by telling all his friends about the great Customer Service.

DOC'S PRESCRIPTION: MAKE YOUR CUSTOMER SERVICE GREAT

Now let's think about the service your Customers get, and whether you're fully meeting their wants, needs, and demands.

Think about the processes you have in place, and think back to what you hear frequently from customers. Based on this, rate the current Customer Service experience you provide on a scale of 1 to 10 (with ten being the best).

    1   2   3   4   5   6   7   8   9   10

What things do you think you're doing right when it comes to Customer Service?

_____
_____
_____

What do you think is your weakest area in Customer Service?

_____
_____
_____

In what ways have you turned Customer Service into "Customer, Serve Us"?

_____
_____
_____

How are you "baking in" Customer Service when it comes to the product, service, or knowledge that you offer?

_____

_____

_____

In what ways have you neglected Customer Service in your offerings and left it for the end?

_____

_____

_____

Think about walking through the front door of your own business, dialing your own business's number, or visiting your own business's website. How is your Customer Service?

_____

_____

_____

What aspects of the Customer Service would you change?

_____

_____

_____

Are any of your current Customer Service practices more company-centric than customer-centric?

☐ Yes   ☐ No

If any are, how can you change them to deliver value to the customer?

_____

_____

What are you doing to take care of the Customers you have?

_____

_____

Name two more things you can start doing to make sure you're keeping your current Customers happy.

1. _____

2. _____

What can Customers be certain of every time they do business with you?

_____

_____

What do you *want* Customers to be certain of that they may not be today?

_____

_____

What can you do to increase certainty in these areas?

_____

_____

Are you training your representatives to say yes, or to say no?

_____

_____

What is one thing you can start saying yes to?

_____

_____

Do you treat your Customers like your best friends?

_____

_____

Are you "buffing out" regular and new Customers alike?

_____

_____

When you have an awesome Culture and engaged, empowered employees, giving your customers the best service will come naturally. Now that we've pumped up your Customer Service and understand how important it is to treat customers like they matter, let's move on to the next key aspect of Culture—your Brand.

10
BRAND

This is what they say about us.

Objective:

To examine your company's Brand—the identity of your company, which is the end result of any company's Vision, Purpose, Business Model, Unique/WOW Factors, Values, and Culture.

Say you know a guy named Jim. Jim wants to be known as an honest, likeable guy. But what if Jim is constantly ripping off customers and friends? What if he's passive-aggressive and rude half the time? No matter how badly he wants to be known as this honest, likeable guy, he'll never get there—he'll never be able to change his personal Brand—unless he stops these behaviors.

This may seem obvious, but the same principle applies to companies—and yet many act as if it doesn't. I've seen too many companies try to "rebrand" themselves without looking at changing the way they conduct their business on a day-to-day basis.

Ironically, your Brand is the last thing you should attempt to change, because it is the result of everything else you have been doing. You can't just create a Brand, nor can you create a reputation. Both are built over time by what you do and how you do it.

Your Brand is your identity and reputation, and it's mostly the end result of your company's Vision, Purpose, Business Model, Unique/WOW Factors, Values, and Culture—all of which you've worked on so far in this workbook. But you cannot, like Jim, say that your Brand is one thing when all these factors point to it being something else. That's because a Brand is what *customers* say about you, not what *you* say about you.

The shortcut to finding out your company's Brand is to ask these questions:

- What do your customers say about you?
- What do they think of your company?
- What do your customers say you are?

We'll have you answer these and other questions about your own Brand at the end of this section, but first, let's explore six principles of great Brands.

1. GREAT BRANDS ARE ALIGNED WITH EVERYTHING THE COMPANY DOES

As we mentioned before, your Brand is the result of what you're currently doing. You can't hire a Brand manager and expect her to give your company a superficial revamp that solves your branding problem. You can't say, "This is what we want our Brand to be," but have your Vision, Purpose, Business Model, Unique/WOW Factors, Values, or Culture out of alignment with that desired Brand.

Imagine that Stan of Stan's Fruit Stand decides that he wants to strengthen the company's Brand by bolstering their reputation for fresh, local, organic fruit and vegetables. But what if quality has lapsed and the company has moved away from its Vision and Purpose (*"Providing the finest-quality fresh organic fruits and vegetables"*)? What if customers come in to find wilted lettuce and brown bananas? What if the stand features no offerings from local organic farmers?

If that's the case, Stan can't just create a new logo, print brochures, and create new advertisements that support the desired Brand. He has to go back and align what his business is doing. Right now he's not living up to his Vision, Purpose, Unique/WOW Factors or Values, so he has a serious misalignment. He can't possibly resurrect the Brand without going back and aligning every part of his business with the structures of the Culture.

Think about your company. Is any part of your structure (Vision, Purpose, Business Model, Unique/WOW Factors, Values, or Culture) out of alignment with the Brand you want? If so, explain here:

_____

_____

_____

2. GREAT BRANDS ARE ALIGNED WITH THE WANTS, NEEDS, AND DEMANDS OF EMPLOYEES

Since your Brand is the result of what you do and how you do it, the best place to start the process of working on your Brand is with employees. Whatever you want your Brand to become, have your employees live and breathe it first. The Brand inside your company creates the Brand outside it.

If you want your customers to Brand your company as one with great service, but you treat your employees badly, do you really believe that your employees will deliver great service?

Maybe, but that will last for only a short time because employees who are treated poorly will eventually treat the customers the same way they are treated.

Let's say that Shair wants to polish its reputation as a company that connects people, bringing them together around its state-of-the-art app platform. (Remember that the company's Vision and Purpose is *"Bringing people closer to the magic of entertainment by empowering relationships."*) But what if it treats its internal staff like slaves, relegating them to a depressing cube farm and penalizing them when they interact socially while on the clock? That's a pretty severe misalignment; employees who don't feel connected to the company or their colleagues will never help build the Brand this company wants.

Think about the Brand you want your company to have—what you want your customers to say about you. Are your employees living it every day? (If they're not saying what you want to hear, you'll never hear it from customers.)

Do your employees currently live and breathe your Brand? If not, what can you do to change this?

_____

_____

_____

3. GREAT BRANDS ARE ALIGNED WITH THE WANTS, NEEDS, AND DEMANDS OF CUSTOMERS

Of course, your Brand needs to be aligned not only with your employees but also with your customers. (Remember—their ongoing business is what allows you to fuel the Culture!)

Let's say that Northeastern Data hires a new Brand manager who wants to alter the Brand to emphasize that the company is hip, cool, and fresh. There's nothing wrong with this in theory, but is that what customers want, need, and demand? What if the company's customer base would prefer the Brand to be more focused on safety and security—in alignment with its Vision/Purpose, *"Protecting What Matters"*—than on hipness? Well, all that work on the Brand would be wasted. You might have a cool Brand, but it's not speaking to your customers nor aligned with the original structures of your Culture.

Is your Brand in full alignment with the wants, needs, and demands of your customers? If not, how could you realign your structure to create a Brand that is in alignment?

_____

_____

_____

4. GREAT BRANDS KEEP THEIR MESSAGE SHORT AND SWEET

Just as the Vision, Purpose, and Values need to be short and clear, you need to create concise and repeatable messaging for your Brand or what you want your Brand to be.

Pick a couple of words, a saying, or an experience that you want your customers to remember and repeat. This would become your Brand.

One pistachio company did this very well, distilling its Brand message into three short phrases:

Lowest-Fat Nut

Heart Healthy

Get Crackin'

That short-and-sweet message convinced me pistachios were a good snack option. And since the message of the commercial is easy to remember and repeat, I can let my friends know as well. It's great word-of-mouth!

Can you distill your Brand message into a few words or phrases that, like your Vision, Purpose, and Values, are short, clear, and easily repeatable?

_____

_____

_____

5. GREAT BRANDS CREATE AN EMOTIONAL CONNECTION

Great Brands show customers (and employees) that the company is doing more than delivering a service, product, or knowledge; they instead create an emotional connection that keeps people loyal and coming back for more.

Take Southwest Airlines, for example. This company has built a Brand centered on timeliness and friendly service. I don't particularly feel like a high-roller when I fly Southwest, but I know I can count on my flight departing and arriving on time, and on being treated like I matter. The punctuality is great, but it's the emphasis on friendliness and caring service that creates the emotional connection between passengers and the Southwest Brand.

If your Brand successfully creates an emotional connection like this, people will be drawn to you; they will think of your company not as a cold, faceless institution but as a trusted friend.

Does your Brand create an emotional connection between the company and its employees and customers? If not, what can you do to change this?

_____

_____

_____

6. GREAT BRANDS ARE TRUSTWORTHY AND CONSISTENT

A Brand should allow customers to know what to expect when they do business with a company. As discussed at the beginning of this section, we can market our Brand to look good in brochures, but if what is delivered doesn't live up to the hype, we won't be around for long—people won't find the Brand trustworthy.

A Brand also needs to elicit predictability and repeatability. Customers need to know what they can expect anytime they choose to interact with your company. McDonald's gets this right: You can walk into a McDonald's in any city and feel confident that you are going to get the same food you would get in your hometown. The company's procedures have ensured this consistency and trustworthiness.

Coca-Cola, on the other hand, learned this the hard way back in the 1980s, when the company changed its formula from Original Coke to New Coke. The backlash was so intense that the formula had to be changed back. Customers were dismayed that the Brand had failed to be consistent, and they protested in droves. (Coca-Cola was smart to switch back—otherwise they would have been out of alignment with the wants, needs, and demands of their customers.)

Do customers see your Brand as trustworthy and consistent? Do they know they can count on you to deliver what they want, time and time again?

_____

_____

_____

DOC'S PRESCRIPTION: MAKE YOUR BRAND GREAT

Now let's take a closer look at your Brand. By answering the questions below, you'll assess where you're at now and what you need to do to take your Brand to the Next Level.

Briefly describe your desired Brand using a few words and phrases:

_____

_____

_____

What are customers saying about you? Does it match the description of your desired Brand?

_____

_____

_____

If there is a mismatch between the Brand you want and what customers say about you, what do you need to do to influence customers' comments?

_____

_____

_____

In the first part of this section, you assessed whether any part of your structure—Vision, Purpose, Business Model, Unique/WOW Factors, Values, or Culture—was not aligned with the Brand you want. If you found that one was indeed not aligned well, what can you do to fix this?

_____

_____

_____

THE BRAND CHECKLIST

You've now done some deep thinking about your Brand. Run through the following checklist and see if you have any areas you still need to work on.

Does your Brand . . .

- ☐ Align with everything your company does, including your Vision, Purpose, Business Model, Unique/WOW Factors, Values, and Culture?
- ☐ Align with the wants, needs, and demands of employees?
- ☐ Align with the wants, needs, and demands of customers?
- ☐ Keep its message short and sweet?
- ☐ Create an emotional connection?
- ☐ Show customers that you are trustworthy?

Did you miss any? If so, write the steps you're going to take to resolve the issue:

_____

_____

_____

_____

Do you have a plan in place? Now, restate your Brand message in a short, clear, and memorable way:

_____

Way to go! Getting your Brand nailed down is a huge accomplishment, and a crucial part of keeping your company Culture strong. We have just one key aspect of Culture left now—Experience and the Emotional Connection.

11
EXPERIENCE AND THE EMOTIONAL CONNECTION

This is the pot of gold if we do it right.

Objective:

To create a phenomenal Experience for—and an Emotional Connection with—your employees and customers.

We've now arrived at the most important part of your business: Experience and the Emotional Connection. This is the place where everything should all come together. This is the reason we have created the Culture in the first place and why our people have brought it to life. Because, beyond everything we have talked about, it's the Experience that matters most. Everything we've worked on so far—from Vision to Leadership to Customer Service—builds to this point.

We've all heard people say, "I love this place . . . that restaurant . . . this doughnut . . . that person . . . this company." We love these things because they make us feel great. If you create an Experience that makes employees and customers feel great, you have won the battle. You have elicited an emotional reaction and created an Emotional Connection—and kicked off the process of retaining their love and attraction. Everything you have read in this book is about directing all of your efforts to providing the best Experience possible.

WHY IS IT ALL ABOUT THE EXPERIENCE?

When staff and customers are having a great Experience, and we keep it up, we will have loyal employees and customers who attract even more employees and customers.

This is because the great Experience an employee or customer has creates an emotional reaction; that reaction forms an Emotional Connection, and the memory of this connection keeps brining that person back to your company. Through the great Experience you provide, people condition themselves to come back again and again.

If we create a bad Experience, though—say a customer is snapped at by an employee, or bites into a piece of grilled chicken that's still cold inside—we're still creating an Emotional Connection, yet it will be a bad one. Once we have a bad Experience that creates a negative Emotional Connection, we as customers are likely to permanently steer clear of the company that gave us the bad Experience.

It's how our brains work; it's how we are wired. The area that is responsible for the formation and storing of memories from emotional events is located in the limbic system, in a place called the amygdala. And memories are not necessarily formed by a single emotional event; they can be, but they are usually patterned or conditioned in the brain over time by repeated Experiences.

But it's only the really great or really bad experiences that create emotional reactions.

There's no spark for so-so, expected, or merely good or satisfactory Experiences.

A regular experience that merely satisfies—a so-so experience—doesn't elicit any kind of emotion or emotional reaction, so there is no Emotional Connection, because there is nothing to remember, nothing that will harm us or help us; we have therefore evolved to not remember those Experiences. There is no spark for ordinary or expected events or Experiences. It's a pretty simple evolutionary process.

I'm sure we have all been asked if we ate at this restaurant or shopped at that certain store, and we have replied, "I think so, but I can't really remember." That's because it was a so-so, mediocre, or just satisfactory Experience . . . it didn't form any memory, because there was nothing worth remembering, and we don't even remember to ever go back. On the other hand, great or horrible Experiences, those that get us excited or upset, help us or harm us, do spark an emotion and an emotional reaction—and will create an Emotional Connection through our memories.

PRINCIPLES OF GREAT EXPERIENCES AND EMOTIONAL CONNECTIONS

Before we explore the Experience your company is giving and the Emotional Connection it's creating with your customers, let's discuss three important principles to keep in mind.

1. Start with Employees

As we've discussed elsewhere in this workbook, the best way to make sure your customers are being treated to great Experiences is to treat your employees to great Experiences. If you create the great Experience and Emotional Connection for employees, they'll deliver it to customers.

What if Northeastern Data was committed to gaining a positive Emotional Connection with customers by giving them the safest data storage and the best user interface—the best overall Experience—in the industry. But what if, at the same time, the company was headquartered in a depressing, run-down building, where low-pay employees sit in drab, gray cubicles. How on earth will employees having such a terrible Experience enable customers to have an outstanding one? The answer is, they won't—ever.

If Northeastern Data truly wants to give customers the best Experience, it will make sure that Experience is rooted in the day-to-day lives of its employees.

Do your employees have a great Experience working for your company? Is it outstanding, or is it so-so or blah? Is their Emotional Connection positive or negative? Is it outstanding, or is it so-so or blah?

_____

_____

_____

_____

2. Pay Attention to the End of the Experience

The last thing the customer Experiences heavily "colors" his or her memory of your company. What happens at the end is so important that you should not only focus on the overall Experience but also pay close attention to the last part of the Experience.

Imagine that Shair decides it wants to create more word-of-mouth, and someone comes up with the idea of asking current customers for referrals. The company implements a plan: After a customer has bought three Shair apps, he or she automatically gets an email that reads: "Dear Customer, We noticed you've been enjoying our applications. Would you do us a favor and tell three friends about your Experience with the Shair platform and the apps hosted there? We'd appreciate it!"

Not a good idea. Shair could've given the customer the best Experience possible—sleek, intuitive platform; high-quality, useful applications; cross-functionality with every device the person owns—but this one little email at the end of the sale could cause that all to come crashing down. The company is asking the customer to do work for the company's benefit, and that's not part of a stellar Experience.

Instead, Shair would have been better off to trust the process of creating word-of-mouth in the Information Age. If the company sets up a great Experience, the Emotional Connection and memory that are created will encourage customers to share the news on their own (and you can count on this to happen now that we're in the Information Age). Shair should simply sincerely thank customers for their business, or even give them some sort of added value at the end of the Experience, instead of tainting the perception by asking the customer to do work.

The same goes for up-sells and surveys—avoid these at the end of the Experience; otherwise, you may dampen the effect of the entire process.

Does your company do anything at the end of the Experience that compromises the Emotional Connection you are trying to make? If so, what can you do to eliminate this element of the Experience? And what can you replace it with that will add value to the overall Experience?

_____

_____

_____

_____

3. Don't Ruin the Experience by Skimping

Emotional Connections seem to last forever, and some continue for a lifetime, so keep that in mind the next time you think about increasing your profit margin by decreasing quality or customer service. Too many companies let a ten-cent decision ruin the customer Experience.

When companies skimp on the experience because they want to save a fraction of a dollar, they risk making no Emotional Connection ("Meh, my Experience was mediocre") or—worse—making a negative Emotional Connection ("This Experience was terrible, and I'm going to mention it to all my friends!").

It's important to remember that giving customers a fantastic Experience is far more valuable than saving a few cents. Your losses due to the fallout from that poor Experience will far outweigh your savings.

Imagine that Stan decides to save a little money by getting rid of some of the employees who prepare, restock, arrange, and are responsible for the presentation of the fruits and vegetables. Stan justifies the move because his profit margins are smaller than those of "regular" markets—why should he make less money than "regular" markets that don't provide the *finest-quality fresh organic fruits and vegetables*?

Stan figures that when the cashiers aren't busy, they can prepare, restock, arrange, and create the presentation of his produce, reducing his overhead and increasing his profits. Well, in reality, Stan's Fruit Stand has been very busy for years, and the cashiers don't have much downtime. Plus, they aren't trained in the proper preparation and presentation of produce.

Over time, Stan's once-beautiful produce displays start to wane. Instead of the attractively arranged produce of the past, the presentation now looks poor and under-stocked. The fresh organic corn that was once individually manicured to look fantastic now looks like it has been dumped out of a large container. The lettuce is the same way—the outside leaves that were once trimmed to perfection are now wilted, ragged, and tired looking. The entire selection of produce looks as though it has been picked over, like something you'd see in a flea market.

Even though Stan is providing the same *finest-quality fresh organic fruits and vegetables* as before, the Experience was compromised by the poor presentation. Feeling betrayed by a once-trusted merchant, customers form a negative Emotional Connection—and you bet they're going to tell their family and friends about it.

Stan sure saved some money in the short term, but over the long haul, the overall Experience went straight downhill, just like his business, thanks to the reduced following of formerly loyal customers.

Is your company skimping in an area of your business that damages the Experience and Emotional Connection—whether with employees or customers? If so, explain below, and consider the potential benefits of changing this:

_____

_____

_____

_____

Is your Experience in alignment with the wants, needs, and demands of your customer?

_____

_____

Amazon has done a great job of aligning the Experience it provides with the wants, needs, and demands of the customer. With Amazon's huge selection of products, customers knows they are getting the best price, and that their order will be delivered straight to their doorstep. It's a pretty simple model, and it easily trumps that of companies who charge more and force the customer to go out and get the products themselves. Amazon could charge more, but that isn't in alignment with its customers' wants, needs, and demands.

Amazon has gone into other markets and has all but taken them over with the same simple model, which is guided by its Vision: "To be the earth's most customer-centric company." Why does it work so well? Because the markets Amazon goes into are broken—whether the Experience is poor, customers are overcharged, or service is not convenient. Amazon enters the market and creates a solution of being customer-centric by aligning itself with the wants, needs, and demands of the customer, plain and simple.

DOC'S PRESCRIPTION: MAKE YOUR EXPERIENCE AND EMOTIONAL CONNECTION GREAT

What Emotional Connections are you and your company ready to make? Let's find out by exploring the Experience you're currently giving.

Describe the high points of a customer's Experience as he or she purchases your product, service, or knowledge.

_____

_____

_____

_____

What kind of Emotional Connection does this make between your company and the customer?

_____

_____

Are there any parts of the Experience you offer that may not create an Emotional Connection (they are mediocre) or that create a bad Emotional Connection (they annoy, anger, or confuse the customer)?

_____

_____

What can you do to resolve these so that you're forming better Emotional Connections and encouraging customers to come back again and again?

_____

_____

_____

Imagine you have complete freedom to recreate the customer Experience at your company. What would that experience look like, from beginning to end?

___

___

___

___

Did you have any ideas as you imagined this "perfect Experience" that you can incorporate into your current Experience? If so, what were they?

___

___

___

___

Have any of the structures of the Culture you've created so far minimized the Experience and the Emotional Connection?

___

___

What, if any, changes must be made to the structures of your Culture to help ensure a great Experience and Emotional Connection?

___

___

___

___

List two steps you're going to take in the next month to help improve your employees' Experience within the company (remember, this is where it all starts):

1. _____

2. _____

Finally, list two steps you're going to take in the next month to directly improve your customers' Experience:

1. _____

2. _____

Once you have that incredible Experience up and running, you'll be creating long-lasting Emotional Connections between your company and both customers and employees. When this happens, your fantastic Culture has served its purpose, and everything we've worked on so far has come together.

Congratulations! Your company and its Culture have made the shift to the Information Age and are in alignment with the wants, needs, and demands of your employees and customers, and you are making the world a better place.

You should be very proud!

Congratulations!

Now that you've completed this workbook, you've effectively given your Culture—and your company—an overhaul. As you built the five structures of the Culture (your Vision, Purpose, Business Model, Unique/WOW Factors, and Values) and then explored the five key aspects of Culture (Leadership; Human Empowerment; Customers and Customer Service; Brand; and Experience and the Emotional Connection), I hope you had some big realizations about your employees, your customers, and your company as a whole—and what you can do to take it to the Next Level.

You've already done a lot of the hard work, but creating a thriving company Culture is an ongoing process. It's important that you and all the leaders in your company continue to update the structures that support the Culture on a regular basis. The world is constantly changing, and the changes seem to get faster and faster every day; and if you're not vigilant, new trends and ideas can quickly make a crucial part of your Culture obsolete. When that happens, the whole company is compromised.

But when the Culture is vibrant and all its pieces are fully aligned, you'll see beautiful results. Your employees will have their needs, wants, and demands satisfied, and they'll be loyal to the company. When that happens, they'll go on to meet (and exceed) the needs, wants, and demands of your customers. It's a win-win-win—for employees, customers, and the company.